AF584544

LAIR OF ILLUSION

Douglings Adventures: BOOK 2

LAIR OF ILLUSION

Carissa Douglas

AUTHOR & ILLUSTRATOR

PUBLISHED BY
Scepter Publishers, Inc.
info@scepterpublishers.org
www.scepterpublishers.org
800-322-8773
New York

TEXT AND COVER BY
Alston Taggart and Kevin Sample at Studio Red Design

Library of Congress Control Number: 2020945130

ISBN
Paperback: 978-1-59417-403-2
eBook: 978-1-59417-404-9

Printed in the United States of America.

FOR MY SIBLINGS:

FELLOW EVADERS OF THE WOODEN SPOON.

Katrina

Taunia

Allison

and Tyler

Christian
Dad
Liam
Mom
Mary
Lucy
Angelica
Allora
Avila
Jacinta
Serena
Callista
Kiara
Joachim
James

CHAPTER 1

"Don't stop!"

The voice called out from just ahead of her. A tangled web of sharp branches scratched at her neck as she pushed forward blindly, frantically swinging her arms to clear a path. Her breath was labored and heavy; it briefly warmed her chin as a billowing, smoky patch rising in the frigid air before it was quickly absorbed into the dense fog. She turned to look behind her, making out a strange series of knotted trees forming a sort of lair. Was someone in there? She saw a flash of eyes.

"Hurry!" The voice insisted.

She turned back, desperately trying to quicken her pace. Suddenly, she was knocked down. Something was smothering her, breathing into her face. A warm drip hit her cheek and rolled down just below her ear.

"GOOOOD MOOORNIN'!!!"

"UGH!" Allora's eyes flew open and she found herself not in an eerie forest, but face to face with an excited, wide-eyed little girl.

She wasn't sure which was scarier; the bad dream or the realization that the warm blob pooling in her hair was an offering from the drooling three-year-old on top of her.

"Yuck! Callista!" she cried as she raised her shoulder to

her ear. "I love you, but get off of me."

"Gramma's here!" Callista sang. "And she has cookies!"

"Well, that explains the drooling," Allora sighed. "Go downstairs and tell Grandma I'll be down soon."

The little girl climbed off of her big sister and skipped out of the bedroom.

"Did you have that nightmare again?" The voice belonged to her eleven-year-old sister, Angelica, who occupied the top bunk bed. She dropped her head over the side of the bed, her golden curls dangling around her reddening face.

"Yup," Allora answered. "But this time it was a 4-D experience, thanks to Callie."

Angelica giggled. "Life in a large family!"

Allora sat up, reached for her glasses, and then quickly tied her long, wavy, brown hair up into a messy bun atop her head. In her fifteen years of big family life, she was still surprised by how unpleasant it could be to have a boisterous little sibling in place of an alarm clock.

There were thirteen children in the Douglas family, ranging from the oldest, seventeen-year-old Liam, down to the newest addition, Avila, who was seven months old.

"We should go, or there won't be any cookies left for us," Allora said to her sister.

"Cookies for breakfast?" Angelica smiled. "I'm so in."

The girls headed down the hall toward the stairs. Allora swept up a stray two-year-old Lucy along the way, propping her on her hip.

The five-year-old twins, James and Jacinta, were standing by a door in the hallway. Jacinta was trying to pick a lock with a mangled wire clothes hanger, while James, having noticed the two girls coming his way, stood frozen, looking very guilty. The blond little boy slowly reached up and adjusted his glasses before sharply nudging his twin with his elbow.

"Esssuuuse me!" the little girl called out disapprovingly. Her huge, brown eyes looked accusingly at her big brother (he was two minutes older than her). "I told you, we need to get Mary's nail polish to paint your shoes!"

"WHAT?!" Mary's voice could be heard from inside her room. She threw open her door and glared at the two would-be vandals. "Oh, no you don't!" the thirteen-year-old cried. "I'm so tired of you breaking into my room and taking my stuff!"

Jacinta tightened her lips and quickly hid the hanger behind her back. "It was James," she said matter-of-factly. James' blue eyes widened in surprise.

"Uh, witnesses here!" Angelica interjected, waving her hand. "Nice try, Jacinta, but we saw everything."

"Yup," Allora added. "Totally busted."

Mary placed her hands on her hips, her hazel eyes locked onto Jacinta's. "Well," she said, "What do you say?"

Jacinta looked up sheepishly. "Sorry, Mary."

Mary sighed deeply. "I forgive you, but don't do it again. You should also say sorry to James for lying and blaming him."

Jacinta turned to James. "Sorry, Twin," she said. He smiled sweetly and whispered, "I forgive you. Don't do it again."

"Okay," Angelica huffed impatiently. "Can we all just go to the kitchen? We are wasting valuable cookie-eating time."

The children had almost forgotten about their visitor. They hurried down to the kitchen, where their grandmother awaited them with open arms.

"Hello, my sweet Douglings!" she said with a big smile. Grandma was a vision of sunshine: rosy cheeks, smiley eyes, and silvery-blonde hair. The children adored her. She was always chasing the little ones around, demanding extra hugs and teasing Mary and the older children about how cruel it was of them to have grown taller than their grandmother.

"I've brought your favorite cookies," she called out as the children entered. "But don't even think about touching one until you give your old grandma a hug!"

"You need to have some breakfast first," the children's mother chimed in. She was feeding the baby with one hand while attempting to button six-year-old Kiara's dress with the other. "And then," she continued, raising her eyebrows and pausing dramatically, "Grandma and I are going to share some exciting news with you."

"UGH!" Angelica cried out in exasperation. "You know we don't deal well with suspense! Can you please just tell us now?"

"Fine," her mother replied smiling. "Do you remember

Grandma telling you stories about the place her grandfather owned, where she spent some of her summers?"

"You mean *The Castle*?" Allora asked, as she placed Lucy in her high chair.

"What castle?" inquired ten-year-old Serena, who had just entered the kitchen, brushing her long, blonde hair. She was accompanied by Joachim, a husky seven-year-old.

"It wasn't really a castle," Grandma responded. "It was a very large Victorian house that *felt* like a castle. It even had secret passageways. It was up on a great hill, overlooking a lake. There were towers with small windows, where my sisters and I pretended to be princesses locked away. It also had a big wraparound porch, where we stationed ourselves as soldiers on the lookout for intruders. Oh, what a wonderful place it was!"

"Tell us again about the waterfalls," Mary sighed romantically.

"There was a river beside the house. I remember a series of small waterfalls, leading up to a larger one, with huge boulders on either side. We would swim below the falls and then climb up onto the largest rock to lie in the sun. Above the falls was a lush, forested area, and there were several caves near the river, but we were always a little nervous about venturing too deeply into them. It was such an exciting, magical place, it only seemed fitting to call it *The Castle.*"

"Oh, I wish we could go there," Mary said dreamily. "I *need* a castle in my life."

"Wait," Angelica said suddenly. "So, what exactly is the good news you wanted to tell us?"

Grandma couldn't contain her joy. She exclaimed, "My three sisters just bought the property! Our grandfather had sold it years ago and we were hoping that someday it would go back on the market. Well, just last month it did, and my sisters, having lived on their own for the past ten years, have decided to purchase the place and move in together."

"Oh dear," Allora said. "Your three sisters all moving in together? Is that really a good idea?"

Her grandmother laughed. "I know. It's true they are, uhhh..." she hesitated, searching for the right word, "...a somewhat eccentric bunch, but they do challenge each other in a good way, and they definitely make life more...interesting. But I guess you'll be finding out soon enough firsthand."

"WHAT?" Mary gasped. "Are we going there? Oh, please tell me we're going there!" She turned to her mother, eyes pleading.

Her mother smiled. "Yes," she said. "Your dad and I have decided that we'll be sending the oldest seven there for a week this summer. You will be helping the aunts clean up around the property, and assist them in getting settled into their new home."

"Oldest seven?" Joachim piped up. "You mean, I get to go too?!"

"Yes," their mother replied.

"YESSSS!" he cried out before dropping and spinning on

the floor in a sad attempt at breakdancing.

"NO!" Kiara countered. She had been twirling around in her dress, as she was listening to the stories about the castle. "I'm number eight. Are you saying I have to stay home? That's not fair!"

"I'm sorry sweetie," her mother said, softly stroking Kiara's dark hair. "But I'll need your help here, especially with all the older children going away. I promise that we'll try to do lots of fun things here."

Kiara stared at her mother, her blue eyes sad and droopy, like those of a starving puppy. "I still wish I was going," she said.

Her mother sighed. "I'm sorry. I know this is hard for you."

"Going where?" The voice belonged to Liam, who had sluggishly entered the kitchen with the second-oldest, sixteen-year-old Christian.

"To the castle where Grandma used to spend her summers," Allora replied. "The seven oldest are going to stay there with the aunts."

"Cool," said Christian, yawning and scratching his messy brown hair. "I'm driving."

"Nope!" Liam interjected, adjusting his glasses and attempting to deepen his voice. "I'm older; I drive."

"Grandma, do you have any pictures of the castle?" Mary inquired. "I want to start imagining what it will be like to stay there, and it will be much easier if I have an image in mind."

"Actually, yes, I do," Grandma replied, pulling out her

phone. "Come closer and I'll show you."

She pulled up a picture of the beautiful house. She had not exaggerated: it was huge; a mansion. Its brick walls were covered with winding green vines and sprouts of flowers and ivy.

"Oh, how beautiful!" Serena exclaimed. "It's like something from a fairytale."

"You should see the forest," Grandma said, showing them an image of an area with winding, gnarled trees. One gigantic oak tree had fallen, revealing roots, tugged and woven into what looked like a warped throne. The thick branches above had merged and twisted, creating an elaborate, knobby archway. It was majestic, yet haunting. "This part of the wood always seemed to hold secrets," she mused.

Allora gazed at the photo. There was something familiar about it. Something beautiful, mysterious, alluring—and yet, somehow unsettling.

CHAPTER 2

"That's MY wooden spoon!" Aunt Dolly called out.

She had been dancing around in her newly acquired, ginormous kitchen (with aisles that left ample room for her ample hips), but then she stopped and stared at her sister who stood authoritatively over an open utensil drawer.

"I'm well aware it's yours," Aunt Frankie replied curtly. "I want to organize these drawers before the children get here."

"Yes, but I use it ALL the time, so it should go in the drawer beside the stove," she insisted.

"It's so old, it will probably give us all splinters," Aunt Frankie quipped. She remained resolute in her task, as she muttered, "And don't think I don't remember you once chasing our nieces and nephews around with that very spoon."

Aunt Dolly gasped.

"That was a LONG time ago! And it was just a lighthearted threat when they were getting out of hand."

Frankie snorted.

Dolly smiled thoughtfully. "And it must have worked," she continued, "because they're all so lovely now."

"Well, I wouldn't want you to be tempted to pull it out when the grandnieces and nephews get here!"

"Well, then maybe YOU should put away your perfect 'guest' towel. I wouldn't want you blowing your top if one of the children dries their hands and forgets to iron it before hanging it back up!"

Frankie didn't miss a beat. "Don't you know that that is precisely how I'm planning on determining who gets my inheritance?"

"Oh, you two!" Aunt Dot said, entering the kitchen, carrying a pile of boxes rising at least three feet above her head. "Honestly! You both need to stop jabbering and make some room for me, so I can start making my bacon and string bean casserole," she huffed. "The children will be here soon and no doubt, they'll be starving. The last thing they'll want to be subjected to is two old ladies barking at each other!" The boxes spilled out onto the counter, potatoes thumping and rolling about; carrot bunches dropping with a thud. The older, round-faced woman sprawled out her arms on the counter as a blockade. She swept up the stray vegetables and pushed her dark, full curls out of her face with a sigh of relief.

"Who are you calling old?" Dolly asked coyly. "I'm the

baby! I'm GORGEOUS, with years of male-magnetism left in me." She lifted her long, reddish-grey hair with two hands until it was a sloppy mop above her head. She then sashayed dramatically over to the sink.

"That's it," Frankie said sternly. "Do I need to pull out the wooden spoon?"

Dolly stuck out her tongue playfully.

Frankie, normally cool and collected, decided that if ever there was a time for a seventy-year-old woman to chase a silly, childish sixty-three-year-old around a kitchen, it was now, and it would be epic. She raised the spoon, clenching it like a dagger, eyes wild and manic.

Dolly cackled, "You old hen! You wouldn't dare!"

Much to Dolly's surprise, Frankie darted towards her. She was quite fast for a woman who, it would seem, seldom needed to move a finger (for she could manipulate the world with a simple raising of an eyebrow). And here she came, darting at full speed, hissing like a serpent zeroing in on its prey.

Dolly let out a squeal, her tiny feet pattering frantically, her full arms wobbling as she rounded the counter. She bumped into Dot as she was pulling a carton of eggs out of a box. The carton went flying, its eggs sailing out and hitting the floor in a series of splats!

Dolly paused for a moment, thinking the incident would stop the crazed woman's pursuit, but Frankie smiled maniacally and continued the chase.

Dolly gasped, fully believing her sister might actually have gone mad.

She turned and bolted once more, but her fuzzy, pink slippers hit the slick patch of raw eggs on the tiled floor and she went flying, swirling into a dizzy spin until she hit the floor and continued to slide on her backside into a bulky bag of flour that was propped against the pantry door.

POOF! A burst of white filled the air. Dolly, covered with the slimy yellow of egg, rolled into the powder that was still pouring out of the bag. She coughed and sputtered, wiping her face with a hand wet with yolk, as she attempted to catch her breath. She then tried to get up, but slipped once more, face-planting into the ripped bag.

Frankie and Dot stood frozen, mouths gaping.

Slowly, Dolly turned to look at them. She was unrecognizable, her face now smeared with goopy, dripping white paste. She looked like a soggy, abominable yeti.

She breathed deeply. "See?!" she cried. "Totally GORGEOUS!" She burst into laughter, snorted, then coughed from inadvertently taking in more flour.

Dot hunched over, hooting until she was wheezing.

"Oh, you silly goofball! Stop it right now," she protested, "or you'll have me piddling in the pantry!"

Even Frankie was caught up in laughter. In a minute, she breathed deeply and pulled her shoulders back, attempting to calm herself. She even managed to produce a disapproving stare.

"Really?" she said sternly. "So, I guess I'm going to be the only responsible adult for the next week."

Dolly huffed, "You? This is all your fault!" She then whipped a handful of pasty goop at her sister. Frankie ducked quickly, and it hit Dot square in the face. Dot squealed, and then all three erupted into renewed hysterics, as she peeled the sticky clump off of her face.

"Oh dear," she sighed, adjusting her glasses. "We need to clean up this mess before the children get here. And by 'we,' I mean you two troublemakers. I'll need more eggs for my casserole—perhaps I'll get the children to fetch some when they get here. I know I can't count on Frankie to get them."

Frankie huffed, "No, you can certainly NOT count on me. I'm not going anywhere near that coop. The chickens don't like me."

"I have no idea why," Dolly teased, wiping her caked face. "You're so charming."

Frankie raised an eyebrow, silencing her sister.

"Well, the baking will have to wait for now," Dot said. "I'll go get the rooms set up." She grabbed a large bag that was leaning against the stone wood stove. "Hopefully I can trust you two to behave yourselves while I'm gone," she added.

And with that, Dot ventured out of the kitchen, into the foyer and toward the grand staircase. It was such a beautiful structure, all oak, with intricate, ornate carvings and spindles. Dot smiled dreamily as she ran her plump fingers over the banister and looked up at the crystal chandelier. What a gift it was to be back in this magical place. She couldn't wait for her grandnieces and nephews to arrive and share in the wonder that had captivated her in her youth.

She climbed the stairs to the second floor, operatically humming to herself as she traveled down the vast hallway. She came to a small door in the wall; behind it was yet another set of stairs. She trudged slowly up, up, up, until she reached the top step. She stood for a moment, panting. "I remember this once being a much easier climb," she thought out loud. She opened the door to a stream of sunshine. What was once the attic was now a large bedroom complete with an enormous set of French doors leading out to a small balcony. The previous owners had converted the space, and it contained a collection of four beds, two on each side of the room. They must have had daughters, for the walls were covered in wallpaper of tiny rose print. Each of the beds had puffy white duvets with soft, dusty-pink throws, gently laid close to the footboard. Four white posts reached up to a canopy with sheer, light pink fabric flowing down and tied at the middle with golden cords. Beside each bed stood a small, white side table with three drawers.

The walls had been converted into long series of cabinets—drawers, cupboards, and small wardrobes—so that each bed boasted its own cubby, with ample room for each occupant's cherished treasures.

The beams of the vaulted ceiling were painted bright white and from the biggest beam, at the center of the room, a large swing padded with velvet fabric had been hung.

Dot was grateful the previous owners had left the rooms furnished, for this was a vision of loveliness. She sighed deeply. "Perfect," she whispered. "Well, almost." She reached in the bag she carried and pulled out four Bibles, laying one on each of the side tables. "Now it's perfect," she said, smiling.

"Okay boys, you're up!" she said, turning back to the stairs. The east tower stood directly beside the attic, but the access to its upper room (where the boys would be staying) was through a small library on the second floor. The library itself was in the heart of the tower, its circular walls lined with books of a strong variety. From books on Aasvogels (South African vultures) to books on Zythum (Ancient Egyptian beer), there was much to digest.

A black, spiraled staircase of wrought iron rose up through the ceiling, and poor Dot was panting again as she mounted its steps, clinging to the rail. The space above was completely open; no door, with tiny windows along the circumference. The inside of the hollowed, coned roof was lined with thin slats of wood. It was rustic, but clean. Dot decided the room only required fresh linens—and, of course, her choice of bedside reading. In spite of its aged appearance, she knew the boys would love being in the tower. It swelled with medieval charm, and she was sure it would stir their imaginations, just as it had done for Dot and her sisters years ago. She opened each of the small windows, drinking in the midsummer air, and then she turned her attention to the three beds.

All three were captain's beds with three drawers across the base. They sat perpendicular to the circular walls and each was covered with a red quilt with large squares bearing images of knights, dragons, and castles. "This will do quite well," Dot mused as she pulled off one of the quilts and examined it with a smile. She shook it well and set it aside before stripping the bed. She retrieved fresh sheets from her bag and made up the beds, setting a Bible at the foot of each one. She made sure there was one with brilliant pictures for the seven-year-old.

Dot was quite tired after she finished with the three beds. Perhaps if she were not so tired, she would have noticed the large metal trunk pushed up against the wall. It was a curious thing. More curious was the slight movement of its lid, as though it were bursting with excitement (perhaps for the impending occupants of the room), and curiouser still was the small flash of red light that sparked from the rim of its lid when Dot had turned her back to descend the spiral staircase.

CHAPTER 3

"Are we there yet?"

You would have thought that it was one of the youngest children who had asked that for the umpteenth time, but you'd be wrong. It was Mary. Teenager or not, she could almost smell the mystery and allure waiting for them and found the long drive torturous—believing that somehow the miles had managed to multiply themselves, as a cruel conspiracy to keep the most imaginative away from an epic adventure.

Liam's response was a low huff that sounded more like a growl. He kept his eyes forward and continued driving along the smooth road lined with tall, slim trees.

"We could say another Rosary," Allora suggested. "Maybe the Sorrowful Mysteries this time."

"There!" Christian called out suddenly, pointing ahead. Liam slowed the minivan and turned down a long driveway.

The path was narrow, winding, and full of potholes. They could hear the grind of dirt, the snap of twigs, and the clicks of small pieces of gravel hitting the sides of the van. A cloud of dust rose around them, so Liam slowed down, almost to a crawl, and all of the children smiled in wonder as they took in the sight of large, knobby trees wrapped in rich green vines. The branches reached high above them, intertwining and creating a full tunnel with streams of sunshine piercing through small gaps in the lush tapestry of leaves. The forest was alive with small creatures and flecks of color flowering at the base of the trees. The hills rose steeply to one side, adorned with great stones and boulders, some looking as though they had fallen into each other centuries before, creating caves and archways covered with moss and ivy.

"So beautiful!" Mary cried, breathing deeply, and feasting on the enchanting sight.

"Oh, what is that amazing smell?"

"Dirt," Christian stated.

Mary frowned. "I wasn't talking about *that* smell."

"That must be the smell of the ferns, rhododendron, and swamp azaleas that Grandma was telling us about before we left," Allora said. "It's heavenly!"

Liam cleared his throat, which signaled that he was about to demonstrate his vast knowledge of little-known facts—in this case, horticultural ones. "That must mean that we're almost at our destination. Swamp azaleas thrive in partial shade and moist soil, which is exactly the conditions one would find at the base of the falls beside the castle."

A few more twists in the road and Liam's hypothesis was confirmed. They heard the light pouring of the falls, complemented by the gurgling river rushing over the rocks. The drive ended in a small dirt parking lot with a path leading to a large set of black, iron gates. A brick wall lined the property and two large sculptures of lions stood at either side of the entrance.

"Wow!" Angelica exclaimed. "This is so cool."

She jumped out of the van and ran up to the gates, squeezing her face between two rods. Just beyond, there was a grassy area with a picnic table and a fountain. Further on, there was a bridge crossing over the gentle rapids, and further still, there was a stone pathway leading up to one of the most beautiful houses she had ever seen: *The Castle*. It was happily situated on a hill overlooking the waterfalls.

I can't believe we get to stay here, she thought to herself.

She turned back, smiling at her siblings. But her expression soon changed into one of confusion and curiosity. She squinted her eyes and scrunched up her nose.

"What is that?" She wondered aloud, as she stared at one of the great lions.

Something glinted in the sunshine from the creature's open mouth.

"I think there's something in there," Christian said. "Maybe a piece of metal or something."

He reached his hand up, feeling behind the stone fangs. His fingers grazed something cool and slightly rough, in the fold of the lion's tongue. It was hard to get a grip on it.

"There's something here, but I can't quite reach it," he said. "Joa, come here!"

Joachim was happy to help out. Christian lifted his brother onto his shoulders and Joachim stretched his hand up, into the lion's mouth.

"I feel it!" he cried out excitedly. He scooped the item up into his palm.

"I've got it!" Joachim announced.

Christian set him down and held out his hand, saying, "Great, now hand it over."

Joachim pulled his fist close to his chest. "I wanna look at it first," he said firmly.

He peered down at his hand, opening it to reveal the treasure cradled in his palm.

"WHOA!" he exclaimed. "What is this?"

He lifted the small, ornate object, rotating it in the sunlight. He paused, expecting to hear sounds of excitement and admiration from his siblings, but there was only silence. He studied the pale, stunned faces staring intensely at the object.

"What's wrong?" he asked.

"Joa," Serena said softly, approaching him and putting her arm around his shoulders. "You're probably a little young to remember, but that is the same key Allora found a few years ago that opened up a secret door, leading us on a very..." she hesitated, "...life-changing journey."

"WHAT?" Joachim said. "That's amazing! Is that why you guys look scared?"

"Not scared," said Mary with wide eyes. "More like shocked, excited, and a little nervous all rolled into one."

"Oh," Joachim said. "I get it. I remember a little bit. I'm pretty sure I met a Master Jedi, and then I think there was a dark cave..." He opened his mouth to say more, but was interrupted by a high-pitched, happy shriek.

"You're here!!!" Aunt Dolly's voice rang out. The children watched as their great aunt bounced down the pathway from the castle. Her arms were waving in the air in an excited jiggle. Behind her, Aunt Frankie was more poised but walked briskly, her pace as much of a sign of enthusiasm as one could hope for from the stern figure. Aunt Dot followed behind, beaming with joy, and called out, "I hope you brought your appetites!"

"You better let me take that," Allora said to Joachim. "We can talk about this later."

She took the key and quickly shoved it into her pocket.

"Hello, hello, hello," Aunt Dolly blared. "I need hugs!"

The children pushed the gates open and ran toward the bridge, preparing themselves for the impending gushes of affection.

Aunt Frankie was fast on Dolly's tail, hollering after her. "Slow down! Running, for someone with as much extra padding as you, is courting a heart attack!"

Dolly stopped abruptly and turned to her sister with her hands on her hips. "How rude!" She huffed, panting as she continued. "You know the 'extra padding' is because I have a *condition*!"

Angelica outran the others and threw her arms tightly around Aunt Dolly's waist. "I LOVE your condition!" she said, smiling. "It makes for the BEST hugs."

Aunt Dolly turned to her golden-haired niece and laughed. "Good!" she said. "Because I also have a 'needs-a-ton-of-hugs' condition!"

"Well," Aunt Frankie commented, "there's more than enough of you to go around."

"Oh you!" Dolly said, playfully swatting her sister's arm. "We all have a little extra padding at our age! It's God's way of insulating all the wisdom, love, and warm memories we hold.

So just you stop going on about it!" Aunt Frankie raised an eyebrow, but smiled ever so slightly.

Angelica released her hold on Aunt Dolly and then turned to Aunt Frankie, hugging her tightly.

She returned the affection, ending the embrace with a series of five quick pats on the back. The children had always joked that that was "Aunt Frankie Morse Code" for "The-hug-has-ended."

"It's beautiful here!" Mary cried out. "Thank you for letting us visit you."

Aunt Dot caught up to the others. "We're so happy to see you," she exclaimed. "You know who else will be happy to see you? The chickens. After we get your things inside, Mary, Serena, and Christian, you can come with me and we'll collect some eggs so I can make you all a nice, big casserole."

Christian hesitated. "Um, Aunt Dot?" he said. "Chickens don't really like me."

Aunt Frankie perked up. "See," she stated. "I'm not the only one."

Christian smiled. "You too?"

She nodded, saying, "They peck at my fingernails and refuse to lay as many eggs for me."

"I can totally relate," Christian replied. "They peck at my ears when I put them on my head."

Aunt Frankie stared stone-faced at Christian.

Christian lowered his head, realizing the camaraderie had ended.

"Okay!" Aunt Dolly called out, breaking the awkward silence. "Let's get everyone inside! Grab your bags and I'll show you to your rooms."

CHAPTER 4

"WHEEEE!"

Angelica was swinging on the great velvety swing in the girls' room. Of course, she was upside-down, her belly folded over the seat and her hair sweeping the floor. She loved the feel of the blood rushing to her head.

"This room is incredible!" she cried. Serena was holding one of the soft throws against her cheek, as she replied, "It really is."

"You should swing on that properly," Allora advised her sister. "We don't want to break anything."

"I'm not going to break it," Angelica replied. "I'm just thinking, and this position helps me think better."

"Are you thinking about the key?" Serena asked, wide-eyed. "Because I know I am."

"Yes. I'm wondering if we'll have to wait till we get home

and then dig in our sandbox to see if the door is there."

Mary sighed. "We tried to dig it up a couple of years ago. It's gone. I don't think it will ever be there again."

"It's true," Allora said. "There must be a reason we found the key here, right at the beginning of our stay. This must be where we're being called to do something."

"So I guess we should keep an eye open for a new door," Serena suggested.

"Exactly," Allora said.

Mary was sitting on her bed, looking toward the balcony. She sighed, saying,

"I want to be the one who opens the door this time." She jumped up, pushed the two glass doors open, and stepped onto the balcony. "I think I'm overdue for a great adventure." She stood smiling at the beautifully lush forest spread out before her.

"You guys should come and check out this view!" she called to the others.

Allora joined her on the balcony. It was a small semi-circular terrace, lined with a spindled rail. She leaned slightly over the rail and said dreamily, "This feels like a scene out of a Shakespearean play." Allora couldn't help giggling, as she called out, "Romeo, Romeo, wherefore art thou, Romeo?"

There was a deep, somewhat faint, but distinct cough from down below.

Allora froze.

Mary, Angelica, and Serena all ran swiftly to the rail,

looking down, searching the yard.

Mary howled in laughter as she saw a boy of about sixteen looking up at Allora with an amused smile on his face.

Allora's cheeks were burning red. She stiffly edged back into the safety of the room.

Her sisters were all losing it, bent over in laughter.

"I am never going out there again," Allora whispered.

"Why not?" Mary teased. "He was cute."

"We will never speak of this again," Allora replied.

"Except to the boys!" Angelica called out, running to the bedroom door.

"No!" Allora cried, jumping up and chasing her sister. She desperately rushed down the stairs and around the corner, but Angelica was easily the fastest girl in the family, and she was halfway up the spiral staircase leading to the boys' tower before Allora had even made it to the library.

"Stop!" Allora called up to her. "Or you're going to be in so much trouble!"

She could hear her sister's excited murmuring as she mounted the steps, and before she could even reach the top the boys all poked their heads over the rails and called out, "Romeo, Oh, Romeo!" Allora cringed as they burst into laughter.

"Angelica!" Allora roared in anger. "Seriously?! You just had to tell them!"

Her feet pounded the steps, the loud thumping proclaiming her fury.

"It's okay," Christian said, hoping to calm his raging sister. "I've done a lot more embarrassing things."

It was true. Christian had a big heart, but his impulsiveness had often led him to make plenty of open-mouth-insert-foot statements.

"Allora!" Joachim cried out excitedly. "Have you seen my bed?"

Allora forced a smile. She was still mad but didn't want to spoil her little brother's innocent experience of excitement and wonder.

"It's really cool, Joa. This whole room is really fun," she said, glancing up at the high conical ceiling. She casually picked up the pillow from Joa's bed, gently tracing her fingers along the seams, before whipping it as hard as she could at Angelica.

Her sister was caught off guard and her face received the full blow. She cried out, "Hey!" But then she added, "Okay, I deserved that."

Joachim laughed heartily, until he had a thought. "Wait," he said, wrinkling his nose. "Did you get drool on it?"

"Maybe a little," Angelica said mischievously.

"UGH!" he moaned. He had spent too much time learning from Mary, so he knew when it was the perfect time to unleash an overdramatic reaction. "DAAAH!" he continued, crinkling his face in disgust, waving his arms, and whirling his body around, as though he'd been caught up in a toxic cloud.

He backed into the large trunk beside the wall and fell onto it. He didn't mind. It was the perfect platform for his final collapse: the sad display of his drool-induced demise.

"Okay," Liam said. "I think we're done here. Let's all go to the kitchen and check in with the aunts."

"AHHH!" Joachim yelped, jumping off of the trunk. He had felt a zap, a sharp surge that left his body slightly tingling. He turned to inspect the culprit, looking accusingly at it while trying not to show how scared he was.

"That's enough, Joa," Angelica said. "No more acting."

"But I wasn't acting," he insisted. "I felt something."

"No more, Joa," Christian added. "It's done."

"I'm not lying! I think that trunk tried to tase me!"

Christian raised an eyebrow and looked suspiciously at his little brother. He then bent down and examined the large metal box, cautiously running his hand over the lid and shaking it. He tried to pry it open, but it seemed to be locked. He found a thin metal piece where the latch would normally be, which slid to one side. When he moved it over, it revealed a small panel with five buttons, each bearing strange letters.

"Liam?" Christian called out. "Any thoughts on this?"

Liam adjusted his glasses and squinted his eyes as he brought his face close to the panel.

ΣΥΧΘΙ

"Weeeird." The word poured out slowly as he googled his mind.

"These letters look familiar. I think they may be Ancient Greek, but I am not quite sure why they are in this order."

"Maybe the key is to push them in the right order, maybe it's a message or something," Christian offered.

"We may have to leave them for now," Allora advised. "Something tells me that everything will make more sense once we figure out why we were sent the key."

"Yes," Angelica agreed. "And maybe when we find the door!"

"What door?" A panting Aunt Dot's head bobbed into view as she entered the room.

"Uhhh..." Angelica wasn't quite sure how to answer. She didn't want to share about the key quite yet, but also didn't want to be deceitful.

Aunt Dot sighed. "Oh, do you mean the door for this room? You must have noticed the hinge markings on the floor by the opening. I remember there used to be a panel-type hatchy thing that lifted up, but the last owners must have removed it. I realize that it may create a bit of a privacy issue, but maybe we can just all call up to you before we climb the stairs." She smiled as if satisfied with the suggestion. She then jumped a little, excitedly. "Oooh, and I know how to yodel, so, I could do that. That way, I won't accidentally walk in on you when you're just in your haynies."

Angelica tried not to giggle. Aunt Dot had a habit of making up words.

She whispered to Liam, "I think she means your..."

"Thanks," he cut her off. "I got it."

"Anyhoo!" Aunt Dot continued. "I saw Mary and Serena in the hallway and sent them to fetch the eggs for the casserole. You should all come down to the kitchen and help me chop up some veggies. There's also someone there I'd like you to meet."

Allora winced.

Angelica turned to her sister and grabbed her arm, leading her to the stairs. Allora resisted, dragging her feet.

"Come on, Juliet," she teased. "We don't want to keep Romeo waiting."

Allora hung her head, but begrudgingly followed her sister.

When they got to the kitchen, they saw Aunt Dolly standing beside a woman of about sixty. She had a short, white, wavy bob cut and stylish, purple glasses with gem-studded arms. She had a beautiful smile and twinkling brown eyes with flecks of gold.

"Hello!" she said happily. "I've heard so much about you all!"

Angelica leaned into Allora, whispering, "Romeo doesn't look like himself."

"Stop it," Allora threatened under her breath, as she squeezed her sister's arm.

She was relieved, and yet somehow a little disappointed.

"This is one of our dearest friends, Pam Stevenson," Aunt Dolly proclaimed. "She's so lovely. She owns the garden nursery in town and has been helping us with some of the gardening around the castle."

Pam beamed. "It's such a treat to be here. It's an incredible property with so much potential."

The door from the porch to the kitchen suddenly burst open. Allora's heart flinched as a young teenaged boy came in. He glanced quickly around the room before smoothing out his thick, dark, tousled hair. "I'm sorry to barge in," he said sheepishly. "I didn't mean to startle anyone." His bright blue eyes met Allora's.

"That's okay," Pam said. "But I thought you had to head back into town. Frankie was going to give me a ride home."

He shrugged his shoulders. "Change of plans."

"This is my grandson, Will," Pam said, gesturing her hand toward the tall young man, who couldn't seem to stop smiling.

BANG!

He jumped forward a little, as Mary and Serena abruptly pushed the door behind him, banging it against his back. "Oh, sorry!" Serena chirped from the other side of the door. "We didn't know anyone would be standing there."

They were out of breath from having raced back from the chicken coop while trying not to break any of the fresh eggs they had collected. Their eyes widened when they noticed the young man rubbing his back from the impact. "No worries," he said reassuringly. Serena tried to walk by casually, keeping her focus on Aunt Dot as she presented the basket to her.

Mary was less conspicuous in hiding her interest in the

visitor. "Hi," she sang, smiling profusely.

One by one, the children introduced themselves. He nodded politely at each member, but when Allora spoke her name, his smile grew larger as he repeated her name.

There was a light fluttering in her stomach. Her cheeks started burning again and she lowered her head, hoping her hair would veil her face.

"Well, since Will's here, it might be a good time to give the children a bit of a tour of the property," Aunt Dolly suggested. "Will has been doing a lot of work in the gardens by the falls. He's been such a godsend since we moved here. He'll be able to show you the paths leading to the forest and can point out the areas that have poison ivy."

"Yes!" Aunt Dot interjected. "Because, trust me, you do not want to go swimming in the lagoon, and then accidentally sit under the wrong tree, and end up with a rash on your woddler! I learned that from experience."

"That sounds great!" Angelica said excitedly. "I mean the tour of the property...not the rash on your...woddler."

She tried to stifle her giggles. It didn't work.

"I'm up for that," Will said, still smiling.

CHAPTER 5

The fragrant breeze was a warm welcome for the children. Serena spread out her arms and spun around gracefully. Joachim discovered a small, speckled frog and was insistent he could speak the language. He held the small creature up to his ear. "What's that, my little friend?" he said sweetly. "Oh, I see."

"This guy wants to go to the river," he said, holding his energetic companion captive in his cupped hands. The frog's tiny feet gently but frantically scraped the inside of Joachim's palms. "Hey! That tickles!" he giggled. "I think I should name you Wriggle McSquiggles."

"You can't keep him," Allora asserted.

"I know," Joa sighed, "but I do want to find him the perfect home."

"Well," Will said. "Do you think Wriggle McSquiggles

would like to start his house-hunting at the waterfalls?"

"Definitely," Joachim replied excitedly.

"Oooh, I second that!" Mary added. "I didn't get to have a good look at them yet. Can people swim through the falls?"

"Yes," Will answered. "They're pretty gentle. You can easily swim under them and, for anyone who's brave enough, it's also possible to jump down from the top. The falls are only about ten feet high and the water beneath is pretty deep."

"I can't wait to do that!" Mary replied.

"Do you want to see something really cool?"

The children all nodded and followed Will down the stone path leading to the river. The light mist of the water-falls moistened the air, mingling with the sweet aroma of the azaleas. Within minutes the group witnessed one of the most beautiful sights: the cascading falls pouring gently into a turquoise lagoon. They were surrounded by giant boulders layering and projecting out over the water. The children stood motionless, held in a thrilling silence.

Joachim bent down and released Wriggle McSquiggles, who hopped happily into the water with a muted splash. "Goodbye, my friend," he whispered sadly. "I'll never forget you."

"Over here," Will motioned to the group. He led them around a large boulder and along the lip of the water's edge. The wall behind the falls looked like giant slabs of rock, layered tightly, with deep erosions.

"There's a hidden cave that curves behind the falls," he

said in a suspenseful tone. "Is anyone interested in checking it out?"

His suggestion was met with unanimous approval.

He approached the wall and slid his hand between a sheet of green, weepy foliage dangling down from the crest of the falls. As he parted the delicate, leafy drape, the small entrance to a cave was revealed.

"Whoa!" Angelica cried. "Does anyone else know about this cave?"

"I'm not sure," he answered. "I'd be surprised if anyone spent much time exploring here because of that." He gestured toward a patch of wild grass and greenery that sat to one side of the entrance."

"What is it?"

"Poison ivy."

He raised his eyebrows. "You'll have to be careful not to get too close to it. You wouldn't want to deal with a rash on your woddler." He chuckled and Angelica snorted.

He lowered his head and crouched down as he crept into the mouth of the cave.

"I'm a little claustrophobic," Allora called out, hesitantly. "Tell me it gets bigger in there."

"It does!" Will's muffled voice called back. "Much bigger!"

"Okay," she said with a determined voice. "Then I'll go next."

She hunched over and pushed the green veil aside, quickly working her way through the entrance. Will took her hand and pulled her up into the large cavity beyond.

Her stomach fluttered furiously.

"I thought it would be dark in here," she said forcefully, trying to prevent her voice from trembling.

He smiled and, with some reluctance, released her hand. "There are a few openings in the wall behind the falls. They're high up, but you can see the back of the falls through them, and on sunny days it can get quite bright in here."

The chamber was an eight-foot-high semi-domed area. It was a surprisingly large space: about twelve feet deep and fifteen feet wide.

Allora's eyes swept over her gray-stoned surroundings, delighting in the prismatic colors dancing on the back walls: a playful effect of the light through the waterfalls. Her expression of admiration remained as she turned back to Will, who was enjoying her reaction to the secret cavern. He couldn't help feeling proud to have been the discoverer and the one to elicit such a favorable response from his new companion.

"Wow!" Liam's voice bellowed as he entered the cave. The two jumped at the sound of his voice.

"This is amazing! Although with several more years of erosion, the falls could collapse into this void. That would be quite the sight."

Allora looked quickly away from Will.

Liam frowned awkwardly. "Um, I hope I'm not interrupting anything..."

Now it was Allora's turn to frown awkwardly. "No," she said curtly.

One by one the children entered the cave with shrills of excitement. Allora was starting to feel a bit crowded so she slowly backed away from the entrance until she bumped against the far end of the cave. She leaned back firmly, only to jump forward again at the sound of something cracking.

"Uhhhh, Liam—that erosion thing you were just talking about..." Allora said nervously, "Could that be happening now?"

"No. I don't see any evidence of that, so I can't imagine that would be the case." His words were reassuring, but his eyes were wide and darting back and forth.

"There!" Serena called, pointing to the place where Allora had been leaning.

Everyone turned their attention to the wall sitting perpendicular to the falls. The area was fracturing: tiny cracks growing and splintering in sudden, sharp spurts, until the stone surface looked like a dry, desert floor. Bit by bit, pieces of shale clinked as they broke free and slid to the ground, shattering. Then, all at once, the whole section of thin rock dropped like a sheet of broken glass.

Everyone gasped as the sound echoed through the chamber like a clash of mangled cymbals.

Then—silence—save for the gentle sound of the falls still gushing outside. No one could speak at first; they just stood gaping at the wall. For the layer that had fallen away laid bare a large and somewhat familiar structure: two great metal doors. Massive and ornate, they were covered with images of great thorny vines encircling ancient-looking books. Stretching across the doors, the words EX UMBRIS ET IMAGINIBUS IN VERITATEM were gloriously inscribed.

"Liam," Christian said, not moving his eyes from the door. "Translation."

Liam smiled as he reverently adjusted his glasses and cleared his throat.

"It's Latin for...," he paused, *"Out of the Shadows and Images, and into the Truth."*

"I'm so excited, I could scream!" Angelica squealed. "We've found it!!!"

"Finally!" Mary added excitedly.

"Whoooaaa..." Will's voice trailed, as he looked at each of the siblings. "What is happening here? Why do you all seem to know what this is?"

"Because we do," Allora answered solemnly.

"This is a...well, it's a...," Christian fumbled, "a sort of portal, one could say, I guess."

"A portal?" Will asked, fully confused. "A portal to where?"

"It's a place where spiritual realities are rather tangible," Liam stated. "The last door we came across led us to an encounter with a saint who helped us fight off a dark being trying to devastate our family."

Will's eyes were frozen wide, and the blood looked like it was draining from his face.

Joachim poked him. "You don't look so good."

"No," Will squeaked, still resembling a deer caught in

headlights. "Totally fine. Please continue."

"The door only opens if you have the key," Liam continued. "Then, it's probable that we'll be given a particular mission—most likely something quite dangerous."

"You don't have the key, do you?"

Allora answered his question by reaching into her pocket and revealing the curious object.

Joachim was excited. "Maybe I'll get to see my friend again!"

"Wriggle McSquiggles?" Will suggested, lightheartedly, trying to break free from the grip of interior panic.

"No," Joachim laughed. "Old Obi-Wan Kenobi!"

Angelica snorted and giggled, in spite of the thick air of apprehension filling the cavern.

"Let's do this," Christian said, deepening his voice, sounding like a pumped-up superhero.

Allora breathed deeply and approached the doors.

"Wait!" Mary cried out. "Please, please, please, can I do it this time?!"

Allora looked slightly annoyed but handed the key to her sister.

Mary ran her fingers along the surface of the panels, which were cool and slightly moist to the touch. She drew a line down to a small hole, which was encircled by what looked like an iron crown of thorns. She turned to look one last time at the group, smiling, and warning them in a dramatic voice, "You might want to step back."

The others obliged her.

She pushed the key into the opening and turned slowly, before sprinting back to the group and ducking in preparation.

FLASH!

A wave of heat drove the group back further. The doors began to glow and throb. There was a loud mix of rumbling and crackling as an intense, blue flame suddenly appeared at the top and sizzled its way down the long seam separating the two doors.

Then, all was quiet. The doors stood dull and motionless for a moment, before the two panels slowly creaked open.

CHAPTER 6

Driven forward by zeal but slowed by trepidation, the group edged forward. Christian took the lead, with Angelica at his side and Liam close behind. Allora held Joachim's hand. He assured her that he would protect her.

They ventured slowly through the grand doorway, clumped together, trying hard not to trip over each other's feet. Beyond the doors was a great tunnel. Lanterns hung along the walls. They were dark, but as the children approached, each would suddenly ignite, beckoning them to go further. Poor Will was still racked by fear and confusion, but for the others, each fantastical display triggered memories of a world they had once encountered, where nothing seemed fully impossible.

Finally, they saw the warm glow dancing on the walls ahead. A large wooden door stood ajar, and they could make

out the silhouette of a man seated on a majestic red chair with a wooden crest on its back. He sat poised and peaceful in front of a roaring fire.

They froze.

He spoke from the darkness: "I beg you, please, do not be frightened. It would counter the extraordinary elation of my heart: the teeming jubilation of this felicitous meeting. Long have I suffered the seemingly interminable anticipation of your arrival, and now at long last, here you are. So, we must not allow fear to define this most prodigious moment."

He rose from the chair, a tall, slender figure. As he approached the open door, more light filled the room, and the children were met with a deep, genuine smile and kind, knowing, light blue eyes. The elderly man had both a stirring energy and a serene calm about him. He was dressed in what appeared to be a long, black cassock, with a red cape and sash. A matching red cap sat atop a bed of thick, silvery hair.

Joachim whispered to Allora, "He's not a Master Jedi. He doesn't have a brown robe and I don't think he speaks real English."

"He does speak real English," she whispered back. "He *is* English. And those are his cardinal's robes."

"I would not hold you in suspense, for you must find my ancient presence altogether confounding." His eyes twinkled. "But first, please do join me in my chamber. It's quite lovely, with room for all, and there's tea! I'm sure you would agree that a hot beverage is just the thing to warm the spirit and to open the door to good conversation and—with all my heart I would venture to hope—friendship!"

The saint turned to Will. "Oh, my dear boy, your face is quite the portrait of apprehension. You, in particular, look as though you would benefit from some liquid rejuvenation."

The children looked at each other, both amused and astounded. They followed the pleasant cardinal into the room. A large stone fireplace stood at the far side. The walls were not what one would expect to find in a cave but were covered with rich wallpaper, cream in color with burgundy geometric patterns and floral prints. Portraits of saints held in huge gilded frames hung above tall wooden bookshelves brimming with worn-looking texts. Two large, tufted benches sat close to the fireplace, and each guest timidly took a seat, appreciating the warmth from the crackling flames, which easily cut through the cool, damp air. A round, wooden table bore several fine white teacups with flared bottoms and thin, wavy handles painted in gold.

"Fancy," Mary couldn't help saying as she raised an eyebrow and smiled.

There was a tiered silver platter, three layers high, filled with delicate treats: cucumber sandwiches and little tarts and biscuits.

Joachim licked his lips, trying not to salivate.

"Allow me to introduce myself. I am but your servant, Cardinal John Henry Newman."

"*Saint* John Henry Newman," Liam couldn't help interrupting. "I should have known from the inscription on the door: *Out of the Shadows and Images, and into the Truth*. That was the inscription on your..." His voice trailed off and his ears reddened as he was suddenly aware of the awkwardness of citing a tomb's inscription to its deceased occupant.

The saint chuckled.

Liam quickly recovered, blurting out, "You're one of my favorite saints: witty, highly intelligent, persuasive, an incredible writer, and a champion of truth. It is a deep honor to meet you."

"I assure you, the pleasure is mine."

"I am a little confused though," Liam continued. "On our last mission, we were accompanied by a saint who, during his earthly life, could bilocate and speak to angels, and, among other things, was proficient in combatting demons. I mean no disrespect, but if we are entering some sort of battle, wouldn't it be advantageous to have a saint with mystical powers to assist us in combat?"

"I have often found that the pen is indeed mightier than the sword," Newman replied with a wink. "I think you are well aware that the Lord, God of all, is all perfection in equipping his children. There is no error in his having sent me to accompany you on this new journey."

"Liam," Serena's voice interrupted the dialogue. "The tea's getting cold."

"Oh, do forgive me, my dear!" the saint cried. "Yes, lets enjoy this humble spread while we continue our discourse."

St. John Henry Newman served his guests while everyone sat cheerfully poised, for the atmosphere was both warm and regal. Even Will was taken by the saint's kind-hearted hospitality and no longer bore the face of dread. Serena would later describe it as her most favorite "Englishy-quaint" tea party.

Once everyone was settled, Christian blurted out, "Who or what are we facing this time?"

The saint smiled at his frankness. "Yes, I believe it wise to get directly to the point." He grew serious. "There is a darkness in this land, and it has been spreading more rapidly of late. The one responsible is cunning and calculating. His soul festers in greed and selfishness. He is a master of deception, and so skillful is he in luring and persuading the innocent that his lies have solidified into a mental trap for his prey. Many are left despondent until they are no longer responsive to the outside world, but their minds linger in the labyrinth of lies he has created. He has blurred the boundaries of the spiritual and physical worlds."

"Um, let me get this straight," Christian interjected. "So there's someone who's a dangerous liar and manipulator, who's been messing with peoples' minds?" The saint nodded as Christian frowned and continued. "And he's done so much damage that they've been pulled into some kind of maze or mental prison?"

"I know it sounds rather confusing, but yes, that is the gist of it."

"Where do we even begin?" asked Liam.

"At Mass," the saint submitted. "We will open this journey with the greatest prayer. Tomorrow morning, you will attend Mass with your aunts. Beg the guidance of the Holy Spirit, and he will not abandon you. After Mass, you will be brought to a place where you will discover some of the victims. Offer your love, genuine friendship, and service to those you encounter there. They are sorely deprived of heartfelt connection with others, so they will be most appreciative of your time and presence. But you must use caution, for the perpetrator may also be there, and he must not be made aware of your mission. Your safety depends upon it."

"What is our mission exactly?" asked Joachim.

"That, my dear children, will be made known to you at the appropriate time." The saint stood suddenly. "With all my heart, I do not wish to hasten our parting, but I believe your aunts," he said, "and your grandmother," he added, directing his attention to Will, "have been sorely missing your presence. We shall meet again tomorrow after your morning excursion."

As the company quickly finished their tea, the saint pulled Will aside. He smiled sympathetically, his eyes looking deep into Will's. "Do not be reluctant to believe," he whispered. "Do you not know that you have been called here with good reason, to become who you were made to be?" Will lowered his head, not fully certain of the saint's meaning.

The kindly man tapped the boy on the back reassuringly before leading the group to the door and offering them his blessing.

The children begrudgingly left the agreeableness of the saint's charming quarters. Their minds were tingling with mingled excitement and uncertainty.

Once outside of the cave and far from the falls, they heard a strange, offensive sound.

"YOOOOOOOODLE LAAAYYEEEEE AAAHHH

EEEEYYYAAAA YODLE YODLE YODLE!!!"

"What is *that*?" Mary cried out.

"I'm pretty sure that's Aunt Dot's attempt at yodeling," Liam sighed. "Just think, whenever she comes to our room, we'll get to hear it at close range."

"This is the best place ever!" Angelica giggled.

Allora and Will walked behind the others.

"You okay?" she asked quietly.

"I don't know. I think I will be," he replied breathing deeply. "My mind is racing. Did that really just happen? Were we seriously having tea with an actual saint in a place that shouldn't exist? And worse still, are we really going up against some kind of mastermind villain?"

"I know, it's a lot to take in. I was really scared when we first encountered something like this, but it ended up being a really good thing for all of us. I know we're better for it. I guess I'm trusting that that will be the case this time too."

"I keep thinking that I wasn't supposed to be there. This is something for your family. I'm kind of an outsider."

"But you discovered the cave, and you led us there. Not to mention the fact that Saint John Henry Newman seemed to have been expecting you."

"He did seem be expecting me. He even said as much. And when he looked at me, I felt like he really *saw* me, like he could see my heart. It was a bit freaky. I'm just glad I'm not facing this alone," he said shyly, glancing sideways at Allora.

"Yes, I guess we're okay with a rookie tagging along,"

she smiled teasingly. Will's mood lightened as he playfully shoved his shoulder against hers.

"HEY!" Joachim's voice cut in. He had stopped just in front of them. He stood with his hands on his hips, glaring suspiciously at Will, before inserting his body between the two. "I get to walk beside Allora," he said definitively.

"Well, that was one long tour of the property!" Aunt Dot called out as the children reached the castle. "We're having a bit of an emergency here!"

"What is it? What's wrong?" Serena cried.

"The egg casserole is getting cold!" her aunt replied in earnest. "It won't taste nearly as good! Yinz get yourselves in here quick and worsh up!"

"More made up words?" Angelica whispered to Liam.

"No, *yinz* and *worsh* are the Pittsburgh equivalent of *y'all* and *wash*. Grandma's family grew up an hour away from there, so you'll find that there are a few *interesting* words that make up their vocabulary."

"I'm so glad you're good with languages," she sighed.

CHAPTER 7

The next morning, Joachim was the first to rise in the boys' tower.

"WAKEY, WAKEY! EGGS AND BAKEY!" he cried out, as he descended the spiral staircase. "Or maybe it's *BACONY,*" he pondered out loud. He ran out of the library and toward the stairs.

The girls were already in the hallway at the top of the staircase. They happily greeted their young brother and then promptly pried his body off of the stair rail as he attempted to slide down to the main floor.

"Manners, Joa," Serena cautioned.

"Oh, I do that all the time," a breathy voice asserted. It was Aunt Dolly. She was panting as she mounted the steps to greet the children. "It's so much more fun than walking. But I have to make sure your Aunt Frankie doesn't see me. She'd probably break out the wooden spoon again."

The girls and Joachim looked puzzled.

"YUM! What is that glorious smell?" Mary cried out suddenly.

"Your Aunt Dot has been preparing quite the breakfast or maybe I should say breakFEAST," Aunt Dolly answered. "But we'll need to eat soon so we can keep the one-hour fast before Mass."

"Are we going anywhere afterwards?" Allora asked.

"Actually, yes," Dolly replied. "We try to visit Monterey Seniors' Home as often as we can. It's close to St. Anthony of Padua church. We have quite a few friends that live there. Pam's sister lives there too."

"Will Pam be coming with us...or anyone else?" Angelica asked with a mischievous smile.

Aunt Dolly put her hands on her hips and leaned over to Allora. "That Will's a cutie-handsomootie, isn't he?" she sang, teasingly.

Allora scrunched up her nose and dropped her head to hide her quickly reddening cheeks.

"And I thought Aunt Dot was the one who liked making up words," Angelica giggled. "That is definitely one I'll be adding to my vocabulary."

"Oh, look!" Allora called out, gesturing toward the top of the stairs. "A distraction!"

The two oldest boys came clamoring down the stairs, partially oblivious to the small party congregated in the middle of the steps.

"Fooooooood!" Christian blared, storming past them. Liam followed closely behind, offering a quick "Morning!" to Aunt Dolly as he rushed by.

"Teenaged boys and their appetites," Aunt Dolly mused, shaking her head. "We better get down there or there will be nothing left!"

In the kitchen, Aunt Dot was pouring syrup over a mound of pancakes. She was singing operatically, starting with a deep, swirly voice while she held the bottle low over the plate, then growing into a high-pitched shrill (that could rival that of an injured bird) as she raised the syrup high up and continued to pour.

"Aunt Dot is in her element," Aunt Dolly mumbled as they approached the banquet-style spread. "I just wish she didn't have to turn every meal into a musical."

"I kind of like it," Mary admitted. "Especially if it gets her in the mood for cooking."

Aunt Dot had turned to the scrambled eggs, fluffing the light batch with a fork as she hummed a staccato "Chopsticks" melody. She stopped when she noticed the group staring at her with amused smiles.

She was all business. "Fifteen minutes!" she cried out. "That's the cut-off! So, grab a plate, say your prayers, and eat up!"

She didn't have to tell them twice.

After breakfast, the children piled into their van and followed the aunts who were squashed together in Aunt

Dolly's purple punch buggy. Aunt Frankie's disapproval was apparent as she crossed her arms over her chest and muttered, "Honestly, who in their right mind drives something as tacky and juvenile as this. I HATE having to be seen in this thing."

Aunt Dolly smiled smugly, clearly enjoying her sister's discomfort. "I was trying to find a rainbow-colored one with glitter, but alas!"

Aunt Frankie rolled her eyes and sank down into her seat.

"Oh hush, you two," Aunt Dot chimed in from the back seat. "Yinz should be preparing yourselves for Mass, and remember: Father McCranager won't tolerate any more of your disruptions."

"What do you mean?" Aunt Frankie asked, cranking her head around to face her sister. "What disruptions?"

"Giving dirty looks to Edna when she sings off key?"

"Can you blame me?"

"Coughing really loudly when Father is deep in prayer?"

"I thought he had fallen asleep."

"Clearing your throat and tapping your watch when you think Father's homily is too long?"

"That's a functional habit."

"Splashing Martha with holy water?"

"Oh, that was me," Dolly interjected. "She swiped my daily missal and insisted it was hers. So it's not like she couldn't use a good dose of holy water."

"This is what I mean!" said Dot. "Father McCranager

has his eye on you two and don't think he won't retaliate by doubling or TRIPLING the length of his homilies."

"Fine," Frankie huffed.

"It's true," Dolly sighed. "And I guess we should try to set a good example for the children."

"Yes," Dot nodded. "And that WAS Martha's missal. I found yours in my purse and forgot to mention it."

Aunt Dolly's eyes bulged as she peeped, "Oopsy."

At the Church, the aunts were greeted by Fr. McCranager, who eyed Aunt Frankie suspiciously. "I trust your sore throat has healed," he said with a slight frown.

Aunt Frankie opened her mouth to respond but was cut off by Aunt Dot (who was terrified as to what her sister might say).

"These are our grandnieces and nephews," she said, drawing his attention to their guests. "They'll be staying with us for the week."

"Very good," the priest answered with a tight smile. "Welcome. We don't play with holy water here," he added, shooting a look at Aunt Dolly.

"No, we don't," Aunt Dolly affirmed, turning to the children and waving her finger.

Liam didn't miss a beat. "We have a high appreciation of the spiritual effects and corporal benefits of holy water," he said. "We would never misuse or disrespect it. Our dad blesses us with it every night at home, and I can assure you, we have been taught to offer the utmost respect for all sacramentals."

Fr. McCranager's eyes widened.

"We don't drink it," Joachim added solemnly. "Even when we're thirsty."

"Very good," the priest replied, nodding.

Everyone was on their best behavior during Mass, even Aunt Frankie. The most eventful thing to occur was during the sign of peace, when a very confused Martha was hugged by a tearfully apologetic Dolly.

Allora glanced over at a pew across the aisle and saw two familiar faces. They were Pam and Will. Allora's stomach fluttered when her eyes were met by Will's. He smiled and nodded slightly, before lowering his head in prayer.

After Mass, the group caravanned to the seniors' home. It was a large building with a series of gardens surrounding the grey-stoned structure. Although it looked pleasant enough, much of the landscape appeared neglected and sections were overrun with invasive weeds.

"Could use a little of your skills here, huh?" Angelica said to Will, who had decided to carpool with the Douglas children.

"Actually, I'd like to volunteer here sometime," he responded. "It would be good to help fix the place up a bit. My great-aunt, Sophia, lives here and I know she'd really appreciate it."

"Why does she live here?" Serena asked. "Why doesn't she live with your grandmother?"

"She had an operation last year and came here to receive some extra care during her recovery," he said. "I don't know why she's still here. She was doing really well and then she just started getting worse. Now, we're lucky if we come on one of her good days."

"What are her bad days like?" Mary asked timidly.

"On those days," he sighed, "it's as though she can't even hear anyone. She just stares out the window and kind of rambles incoherently." He lowered his head and spoke softly. "It's really breaking Grandma's heart."

"I'm really sorry," Allora said. "I hope today's a good day."

CHAPTER 8

Adele, the receptionist, was very friendly, but also somewhat scattered. She was a slight woman with dark, tight curls and large, warm, brown eyes.

Aunt Frankie couldn't help liking her, as she had a sweet countenance. She used exchanges with Adele to practice patience and mastery over her tendency to give dirty looks.

"FANNY!" Adele called out with a smile. "How are you today?"

Aunt Frankie tightened her face, fighting her default expression of repugnance. She even managed a smile.

"Frankly," she said, pausing for effect, "I'm a little tired today, but happy to see you and the other ladies."

Adele turned her attention to the others. "Hello Dolly, Dot, Pam, Will, and you other beautiful faces!"

"How is my sister today?" Pam asked.

Adele smiled brightly. "You came on a good day."

Pam breathed a sigh of relief. "Wonderful," she said, lifting up a small basket. "I've brought her some treats."

"To share?" Adele inquired coyly, eyeing the home-baked cookies.

Pam smiled and nodded. A voice rang out from down the hall. "I smell something really good!" A woman with long, silvery-white hair tied back in a neat, low ponytail was walking toward them. She had familiar golden-brown eyes and an infectious smile.

"Here comes trouble!" Pam called out. She hurried to her sister, giving her a warm, tight hug.

"You look beautiful," she added. "How did you sleep last night?"

"A little rough," the soft-spoken woman replied. "Nasty nightmares again, but I woke to warm sunshine and happy thoughts in anticipation of a visit from my sister!" She turned her attention to Will. "Where's my hug?" Will embraced his aunt and then introduced the group of children standing with him. She greeted each and then said to the three aunts with a laugh, "My, you have some lovely family genes!"

"I hate nightmares!" Joachim piped up.

"Me too," the kind woman said, bending down to meet Joachim's eyes. "They're wretched things, but there may be one cure ! have yet to try."

Joachim's eyes widened. "A cure for nightmares?"

"Absolutely," she replied with a very serious face. "I've heard that if you pinch the cheeks of a sweet boy of about seven or eight years of age, then POOF, your nightmares will cease to be an issue."

Joachim jumped back holding his hands over his face, giggling. "Nope, nope, nope!"

The old woman's eyes glistened through her teasing smile. "My name is Sophia. What's yours?"

"I'm Joachim, and my cheeks don't like trespassers."

Sophia laughed. "Alright, I'll bear that in mind. We can still be friends though, right?"

Joachim nodded with a smile.

"We're probably a bit too large of a group for my room. Would you all like to come to the lounge area? There's lots of room there and many of my friends would probably appreciate it if I shared my visitors with them."

The children followed Sophia to a large, open area that had enormous windows and several small tables with chairs. A piano sat at one side of the room, where a woman with silvery, wavy hair played a song while humming softly.

The walls were lined with residents; some in wheelchairs, some sitting in the seats of their walkers. A few of the seniors were playing cards and laughing, but many seemed lost in thought, gazing off into the distance.

Angelica sat down beside an elderly man. He was holding a picture that was worn and faded. It was clear that the photo seldom left his hands or his gaze.

"She's very beautiful," Angelica said, looking down at the portrait of a young woman with long, dark lashes and ebony hair.

The man did not speak but nodded sadly.

"Is she your wife?"

He nodded again, tears filling his eyes.

"Is she no longer...here?"

He surprised Angelica by sitting up straight and looking at her directly in the eyes.

"She was taken," he said in a solemn tone.

"What do you mean? Like taken to heaven or like kidnapped?"

He shook his head.

"She's being kept in the east wing. She was moved there several months ago."

"And you haven't seen her? I don't understand. Can't you visit her over there?"

He stiffened his lips and shook his head with a deep frown.

"There's something not right here. She was fine. We came here last year, after my fall. I knew she wouldn't be able to take care of 'big old me' when she already had her own issues with her sight failing and her arthritis always acting up. But Violet was still a sharp cookie. She made our stay here beautiful. Then...she started to change. She was nervous and scared, and soon, she was panicky. She became strange and irrational, going on and on about an enemy inside. First, she said he was inside this residence, then she said he was inside the heads of some of her friends living here. Finally, she said he was inside her head. She was gone after that. She stopped talking and responding to anyone. They told me she needed extra special care and should be kept with the others."

"There are others like her?"

He nodded.

"I still don't understand why you can't see her," Angelica said.

"I did at first. I went over there and sat with her in her little room—more like a cell. She still wasn't speaking. I don't think she even knew I was there, but I still was happy just to be near her. Then, they told me that I was making things worse. I don't know how, but that's what they said. They told me that her health worsened after each of my visits. They said I caused a stressful reaction in her, so, if I really cared about her, I would keep my distance."

Angelica shook her head sadly. "That's terrible. I'm so sorry all this is happening to you. I can't imagine how much this is hurting your heart."

"Thank you," he said, gently patting Angelica's hand. "It feels good to talk to someone about it. I'm Edward, by the way."

"I'm Angelica."

She sighed deeply. "I just wish there was something we could do. It seems so unfair that you don't get to see your wife. I'd like to pray for you and Violet, if that's okay."

"I would like that very much," he said, smiling.

"Can you tell me more about her? Like, what your life was

like before you came here. How did you meet? How did you propose? Do you have children?"

Edward held his hands up laughing. "Okay, okay, I'll tell you all about her. I hope you have a little time and don't mind an old man babbling on."

"I have twelve siblings. I'm used to people babbling on, but usually it's toddler-babble, so it will be nice to hear someone who's actually using real words."

At the other end of the room, Serena had seated herself beside the woman at the piano. Serena recognized the tune being played: "How Great Thou Art." She sang the hymn, while the pianist looked over at her, beaming.

Christian had wondered over to the large windows. The view was beautiful. It overlooked a valley. He heard someone coughing repeatedly behind him, and turned to see a woman hunching over a cane. She had a large bump on her back. She looked into Christian's eyes.

"What are you thinking when you look at me?" she asked.

Christian examined the lines across her soft, leathery skin, her white, wispy hair, her intense eyes and the thin, gold necklace with several gemmed charms laying against her pink cotton nightgown.

"I see someone who has lived a long life, and probably has so much wisdom from all her experiences. Your eyes have seen so much more than mine. I see your necklace and it reminds me of a gift we once gave my mother, each charm meant to remind her of each of us kids. So I see yours, and think that you must be someone who's really loved."

She smiled as her eyes glistened with tears. "So, you don't see an old, ugly woman, whom the world has forgotten?"

"No. I don't," Christian answered solemnly.

"Thank you," she whispered. "He's a liar, but sometimes I forget that and start to believe him."

And with that she turned and slowly started to make her way out of the room.

"Who?" Christian called after her.

She didn't turn back, but lifted her hand above her head, pointing to the opposite side of the room.

Christian looked in that direction and spotted a man in an expensive-looking suit. He was holding a clipboard and surveying the room. Beside him was a small team of people dressed in nursing attire and one wearing a doctor's coat.

Christian saw Pam heading over to the group with a look of concern on her face. He couldn't hear very well, but he could tell that Pam was upset with the man in the suit. She seemed to be asking him questions and he was clearly brushing her off, turning his attention instead to the markings on his clipboard and even holding his hand up in an effort to silence her. The man in the doctor's coat took her by the arm and led her away. He was apologizing profusely.

They headed to the window close to where Christian was standing. Christian turned his back to them, hoping to blend in with the curtains.

"I just don't understand," he could hear Pam saying. "Dr.

Kingsley, you told me she would only be here for a month or two at most after her surgery. Why does her health seem to only be getting worse?"

"I don't quite understand it myself," he replied. Christian could make out a slight British accent. "Your sister was thriving. We were even discussing a plan for her return home. I don't know what happened. I'm so sorry. I know this is very hard for you."

"The director doesn't even seem to care," she added. "I was led to believe this was a home that was deeply invested in the well-being of its patients. Why won't he answer my questions? Why won't he even consider that there's something strange happening here, with so many residents suddenly worsening and losing the ability to communicate with seemingly no underlying health issues?"

"I don't like speaking ill of anyone," the doctor said in a hushed voice, "but just between you and me, I don't think the full recovery of patients is the goal for someone who stands to do well, financially speaking, the longer each resident remains here."

"You can't be serious," she whispered. "These are human beings with lives and loved ones who are worried sick about them. Is it possible that he could be doing something that is inhibiting their recovery...or even worsening their conditions?"

"I've been hearing from many family members and several of the residents themselves, that their loved ones are being negatively affected after they are visited by the director—that their health seems to be rapidly declining after he insists on changes in their plan of care."

"I need to get my sister out of here, now."

"My dear, I need to ask you a huge favor. I believe I'm close to gathering the evidence needed to put a case together to have the director removed, but I desperately need a little more time, and your sister's case is one that I believe will be the most compelling. Would you please allow me just a couple more weeks? We can't allow this to continue. If my suspicions are correct, then many lives are at risk."

"You're asking too much of both myself and Sophia."

"Please. Think of all the families who are also suffering confusion and concern for their loved ones. I'm so close. This travesty has to end. I know I'm asking a lot, but please trust me."

"Just two weeks. My heart can't take more than that."

"I will come through for Sophia and all of the others. Please do not mention anything to anyone. If he finds out I'm investigating this, he'll terminate me and then who knows how many more innocent people will fall prey to this scheme."

Pam nodded silently, though her face was strained with pain.

The doctor took Pam's arm once again and they ventured over to Sophia and her guests, most of whom were seated around a circular table. Sophia seemed lost in thought. Will gently put his arm around her shoulders.

"Hello everyone," Dr. Kingsley said, smiling warmly.

Pam motioned to the group. "We're having a wonderful visit with these lovely people. The children here are the grandnieces and nephews of Dot, Frankie, and Dolly."

Aunt Dolly let out a strange, shrilly giggle. "Dr. Kingsley is the resident occupational therapist here. Doesn't he have the cutest little accent?"

Dr. Kingsley bashfully lowered his head, trying to hide his smile.

He sighed lightly before turning to the group. "I'm so pleased to meet you all," he said.

"Ahhh! See what I mean?" Dolly said, flirtatiously raising an eyebrow. "Doctor, I think your cheeks are getting a little red."

"Perhaps it's but a reflection of the auburn locks that will have me thinking of this pleasant encounter for the rest of the morning."

"Oh, YOU!" Dolly squealed. "Dr. Kingsley and I love to tease each other," she explained to the group. "It's nothing serious." But even as she said it, the children caught her searching the doctor's face for any sign to the contrary.

"You'll have to excuse me," he said. "I have to make my rounds."

"Goodbye," Dolly sang sweetly. Under her breath she added, "future husband." Joachim gave Dolly a confused look. She tightened her lips and whispered, "You didn't hear that."

Mary, who was seated next to Sophia, noticed some strange markings on the woman's hands.

"What are those black smudges on your fingers?"

"Oh," Sophia said looking surprised. "I'm sorry, what a mess. It's conté and charcoal"

"Is that for drawing?"

"Yes, it's a passion of mine. I have a small sketchbook that keeps me busy."

"I'd love to see your drawings."

"Well, if you'd like, you could come to my room and I'll show you my work."

"Yes please!"

"I'd like to come as well, if that's okay," Allora said. "I really love sketching too."

"And I'll come," Will added, much to Allora's delight.

Sophia stood and Mary carried the basket of cookies Pam had brought for her sister.

"A little snack for the road," she chimed.

CHAPTER 9

Sophia's room was a lovely place: a spread of warm touches from someone with an obvious flair for design. Flowing floral curtains and bright colorful cushions added splashes of joy and a punch of personality.

"I love your room!" Allora exclaimed.

"Yes," Mary concurred. "It's so cozy and cheery."

"You can make any place a lot happier with a little creativity and a big heart," Sophia said. "Now where did I put my sketchbook?"

"Is this it?" Will asked, picking up a large rose-colored book from a bulky shelving unit beside her bed.

"Yes, that's it," Sophia replied. "Although, I could have sworn I left it on my side table." She gave a heavy sigh. "I can't trust my mind anymore."

"I can't wait to see your artwork," Allora said. Sophia

perked up. "Yes," she said, "I'll show you some of my favorites."

Will handed the book to Sophia. She sat on her bed and motioned for the others to gather around. As she turned the pages, Allora and Mary were greeted by several charcoal drawings of women in ornate gowns, dancing in a swirl of beauty and grace.

"I *love* them!" Mary cried out. "Are you a dancer as well as an artist?"

"I did love to dance in my day," Sophia mused.

The pages were alive with motion and flight. Allora found the expressions on the figures' faces intriguing. The first series of dancers looked free and spirited, rising above a lush landscape, with clusters of white, soft flowers, but with each turn of a page, their expressions became more deeply pressed with intense emotion. The gestures somehow conveyed a frantic, racing momentum, and strange shadows were etched into the perimeters, almost as though they were closing in on the subjects. The dark forms became more pronounced, and with each new drawing, they were growing into beastly figures.

Sophia seemed a bit troubled.

"I don't know why I drew these. Actually, I don't even really remember having drawn them at all. But I do recall having been encouraged to draw whenever waking from a nightmare...so perhaps I crafted these images while still half asleep."

Allora flipped the pages, looking to see if there was a further progression of the emerging figures, but instead she found stubbled remnants of paper along the seam of the book.

"Why did you rip out pages?" she inquired.

Sophia looked shocked. "I didn't," she asserted. "I wouldn't. I'm someone who will keep even those works that have many mistakes, for I've always felt I can learn something from each of them."

She took the book, and ran her finger along the cropped, fragmented lines.

"There's at least five pages that are missing," she said, still bewildered.

"When did you last draw in this book?" Will asked.

"I'll admit it's a bit of a blur."

"What are your nightmares usually about?" Mary asked with wide eyes.

"I don't really remember," Sophia admitted. "I just know they left me with a dreadful feeling. It's all a bit upsetting, and I don't want to concern any of you. I'm sure all of these strange things can be attributed to my absentmindedness. I know it's been getting worse."

"I have an idea," Will stated. He walked around the room, scanning it. "What if we found a hiding place for your book?"

"A hiding place?" Sophia asked in a confused voice. "Why would I need a hiding place?"

"Aunt Sophia, I don't believe you're as confused as you think. We've all been hearing rumors that something strange

is happening in this place, and I can't really explain it, but I have this strong feeling that your book is being targeted for some reason."

"Will, that sounds a little silly," Sophia said. "As much as I love a good conspiracy theory, I really think this is all related to my moments of feeble-mindedness."

"Would you please humor me?" Will pleaded. "If I'm wrong, then there's no harm done; you'll just have an interesting place where you keep your sketchbook. Please?"

"Okay. Let's hope that I don't forget where the hiding spot is."

"There's not a lot of places to hide things in here," Mary commented as she glanced around the room.

"What about there?" Allora asked, pointing to the wall.

There was a large, thick painting of Jesus surrounded by little children.

"May I?" Allora asked Sophia as she began to lift the frame from the wall.

"Yes, of course," Sophia replied.

Allora flipped the painting over on the bed. It was professionally framed with brown kraft paper lining the back.

"The frame is pretty thick," Allora commented. "I was thinking that we could slice a line through the paper on the back and make a pocket for your sketchbook. Would that be alright with you?"

"Yes," Sophia nodded. "I have to admit that's a really good hiding place. And it will be good having Jesus on guard."

"We'll be coming back in a couple of days," Will said. "We'll check in on you then."

"And I'll make sure I put my sketchbook to good use, especially if I have any more nightmares. I feel even more strongly now about it being a helpful way to deal with all of this madness. I despise living in this state of confusion and forgetfulness, not being able to trust my own thoughts."

Will gave his aunt a hug and the girls followed suit. He

was careful to place the painting back on the wall before leaving.

"We'll be praying for you," Mary said, pausing at the door.

"Yes, please do," Sophia said in earnest. "Oh, and would you please tell my sister goodbye for me? I'm suddenly feeling very tired. I might take a short nap."

Mary had turned to head down the hallway when she bumped into someone, her head ricocheting off a clipboard.

"Oh!" a gruff voice said. "Are you alright?"

Mary rubbed her head. "Yes, sorry. I wasn't looking where I was going."

"Nor was I, obviously," the man answered. "I'm Roger Keble, director of this establishment."

"Ooh," Mary said, sounding impressed. "I'm Mary. I'm a friend of Sophia's family...and Sophia's friend now, too."

"She's a lovely resident. I was just about to check in on her. Was she...able to communicate today?"

"Yes. And she was showing us some of her drawings. She's an amazing artist."

"Yes, I've heard. Does she have any recent work? If so, I'd love for her to show me."

"Well, she's just laying down for a nap now."

"Oh, that's too bad. I guess I can drop by later. Did she happen to tell you if she's scheduled to see Dr. Kingsley today?"

"She didn't mention it."

"No worries. I can ask Dr. Kingsley myself. I should get

back to my office now. I apologize again for the collision. It was nice to meet you, Mary."

"Likewise," she responded with a smile.

She walked down the hall and turned a corner before realizing that she was still clenching the basket of cookies. *Oh no, I should have left these in Sophia's room*, she chastised herself.

She turned back, but as she rounded the corner she noticed that the director was still standing at Sophia's door, staring inside with a perturbed look on his face.

She stopped fast and slipped back around the corner.

"Mary?" a voice called from down the hall. It was Pam.

"Oh good, you have the cookies. I wanted to make sure they were brought to Sophia's room. Let's go deliver them and then head out."

"She's napping now," Mary said, "...and she might also still have a visitor."

"While she's napping? Who?"

"Roger Keble."

"I'm not okay with that. Let's go."

Pam and Mary headed to Sophia's room. Mary saw that the director was no longer standing at her door. Pam hurried down the hall. Mary was a little confused by her quickened pace.

"Sophia?" Pam called out as she entered her sister's room.

Sophia was sitting upright on the bed, staring out the window.

"Sophia?" Pam repeated. "I thought you were having a nap."

Sophia was silent.

"Are you alright?" Pam sat beside her sister, gently placing her arm around her.

Sophia's eyes were wide open. "Lies. All lies," she whispered. "Don't venture too close. They are not what they seem. They bite! Lies! All lies."

"Shhhh," Pam whispered into her sister's ear. "Rest now." She gently laid her sister back on the bed, stroking her hair and covering her with a blanket. "It will all be better soon."

Mary approached Pam timidly. "Is there anything I can do?" she asked softly.

Pam shook her head slowly. "We should go now."

CHAPTER 10

The children sat in silence while eating their lunch in the small but elegant dining room. They could hear Dot humming in the kitchen next to them and could see Dolly's hips swaying back and forth at the door as she leaned over a counter, scribbling something on a piece of paper.

"I hope you're enjoying your cheesy potatoes! I think I could live on those," Dot called from the kitchen.

"Thank you, Aunt Dot," Allora answered. "They're amazing."

Aunt Frankie came into the room. She surveyed the children's plates and wrinkled her nose.

"Dot," she called to her sister. "Are you planning on feeding these children any vegetables while they're here?"

Dot poked her head through the doorway, accidentally bumping Dolly, who turned around with a deep frown.

"Potatoes ARE a vegetable," Dot asserted. "And I'll have

you know that I'm also making my baked beans with brown sugar, mustard, bacon, and ketchup—which, as you know, is made from my homegrown tomatoes... aka vegetables."

"Actually, they're a fruit," Frankie muttered. "And I was talking about the novel idea that people should eat something green once in a while; and I don't mean some over-baked green beans swimming in a cheese sauce."

Aunt Dot gasped. "How dare you!" she called out, before disappearing into the kitchen.

"And how dare YOU!" Aunt Dolly called after her. "You messed up my artwork!"

Aunt Frankie darted in Dolly's direction. Dolly jumped back, fully remembering the last time Frankie lunged at her.

"I'll have to see this *artwork* of yours," she declared, snatching up Dolly's etchings. She let out a hearty cackle.

"Oh wow, Dolly! Or should I say Mrs. Kingsley, Mrs. Dolly Kingsley, Mrs. Dolly Farnen-Kingsley, Mrs. Dolly Ann Farnen-Kingsley?" She shook her head in disbelief. "You've filled the whole page with every possible signature!"

Aunt Dolly snatched the paper from her hand. "The way he's been looking at me lately is a strong indication that I should be making some preparations for my future." She sashayed into the kitchen singing, "Here comes the bride..."

The children tried hard to contain their laughter.

"Wow," Liam whispered, "dinner AND a show."

Aunt Frankie turned to the children, a smirk still plastered across her face. "I can assure you that your 'not-yet-bride-to-be' aunt will be spending the remainder of the day choosing the hymns for her imaginary wedding ceremony. She'll be singing each prospective song both at the top of her range and at the top of her lungs. If you were thinking of spending some time outdoors today, I would advise you to make that time *right now*—for the sake of your ears and your sanity."

Angelica sighed. "Best summer ever."

The children cleared their plates and brought the dishes to the kitchen sink. "Can we wash the dishes and help you clean up?" Christian asked Aunt Dot.

"That's alright," Aunt Dot replied. "Your Aunt Frankie's right. Aunt Dolly is about to get as loud as an opera singer who mistook a Carolina Reaper pepper for a cherry tomato!" She bent over, breaking into a shrill of laughter as the children stood looking a little perplexed.

Aunt Dot cleared her throat and composed herself. "It will be *exploditiously* loud."

Liam couldn't help smiling approvingly at Aunt Dot's newest made-up word.

Aunt Dolly's voice could be heard from the pantry. "Keep talking like that and I won't let you be my bridesmaid!"

"Can I be your ring bearer?" Joachim called out.

"Absolutely, sweet cheeks!" his aunt called back.

The siblings slipped out the side door onto the porch. They were surprised to see a large bouquet of flowers bobbing toward them. Allora easily recognized the dark jeans and pair of blue Converse shoes. She tried not to smile too enthusiastically.

"Hi, Will," she hailed him. He stopped short, peeking out from behind the large, colorful blooms.

"Oh, hi," he replied. "I have a special gift here for someone."

Allora's heart skipped a beat.

"Is your Aunt Dolly around?" he asked.

"Oh, yes, inside the kitchen," Allora stammered, hoping he didn't catch the trace of disappointment in her voice.

"Who are those from?" Mary asked. "A secret admirer?"

"Well, not necessarily secret," Will answered. "There's a card with a name."

He shrugged and headed to the door, knocking lightly before calling out, "Special delivery!"

Liam's eyes widened. "Everybody, plug your ears right now!"

"AHHHHHHHHHHHHHHHHHHHHHH!" The shriek was a cross between a lottery winner and a banshee that had been set on fire. Everyone was surprised the windows were still intact.

Poor Will exited the house rubbing his ears, looking a little bewildered and war-torn.

"I was not prepared for that."

"Sorry," Christian said. "We should have warned you."

"Maybe a little walk will help," Mary said, raising an eyebrow, "...around some boulders, into a cavern behind the waterfalls, and through a tunnel leading to a saint waiting with a hot cup of tea...hopefully?"

Will smiled nervously. "I guess we could try that remedy."

The group headed in the direction of the falls. There was an air of excitement laced with hesitation, for they knew this encounter would bring their mission to light. After meeting with the residents of Monterey Seniors' Home, they understood that this particular adversary had powers over his prey that were both eerie and unsettling. They were loath to discover the extent of his vileness.

Upon entering the tunnel, they could hear the high, soothing pitch of a violin lulling them to St. John Henry's chamber.

Mary sighed delightedly, breathing in the music.

As she entered through the large door, she saw the saint standing in the middle of the room, eyes closed, enveloped in the melodious aura filling the space. He held his instrument close to his cheek, his bow gently gliding over each string, drawing forth what Mary would describe as perfumed notes, rich and heavenly.

"How beautiful," she said. "Did you compose it?"

The cardinal lowered his instrument and smiled deeply. "You have returned. How wonderful!" He beckoned to the others, standing just outside the door. "Please, do come in."

"This piece is particularly dear to me. Though I am not the composer of this delightful melody, it was created to accompany the lyrics to a poem I had written many years earlier, when I was lost, adrift on a ship. Never had I felt so alone, held fast from all I held dear: sick, wearied, and pathetically drained of life and hope. These are the words that pulled me out of the depths of anguish and despair:

Lead, Kindly Light, amidst th'encircling gloom,
Lead thou me on!
The night is dark, and I am far from home,
Lead thou me on!
Keep thou my feet; I do not ask to see
The distant scene; one step enough for me...

There is more, but this particular verse will find you in the near future, when you too have lost your way."

"Are you talking about our mission?" Christian asked.

"I am," the man replied solemnly. "You have met some of the victims and family members that have suffered at the hands of your deplorable foe. I am prepared to reveal the nature of the task to which you are being called. But first..."—he paused, directing their attention to a large silver pot on a table at the other end of the room—"...shall we have some tea?"

The children nodded their heads enthusiastically and allowed the saint to pour each a cup of the warm brew. Joachim tried to convince the Englishman that tea should be almost white and that five teaspoons of sugar was a minimum at best.

St. John Henry patted the young boy on the head and stated, "Here I am, past the stage of my mortal existence, yet I am still acquiring new knowledge...five teaspoons you say?"

"At least," Joachim replied. The saint chuckled and motioned for his visitors to be seated. He sat himself in his red chair and grew serious.

"Soon, you will see the true face of the one who has joined ranks with the fallen angels. Soon, you too will step into the labyrinth of lies. Your adversary's victims are trapped in his maze and will not be able to find their way out without your assistance. That is why you have been brought here: to bring God's light to the darkness, and to break through the shadows and illusions."

St. John Henry frowned as he continued. "This enemy's weapon... is the imagination."

"Wait, isn't the imagination a good thing?" asked a stunned Mary.

"Yes, indeed. I assure you, the imagination is one of the greatest means by which we deepen our faith, but the misuse of imagination—imagination that is not in the service of directing our hearts ultimately to Christ—can be pure deception.

And so, his agent of chaos has been revealed. He has whispered untruths into the hearts of his victims; so twisting their minds, until they no longer see themselves as they are but as he has painted them. He suggested that they were lost and bound, and as his words were spoken, the images of dark, slithering vines wrapping around their extremities solidified in their minds, ensnaring them. He infected each victim's imagination, dominating it and using it to create a prison that has become their new reality."

"So, he sort of hypnotized them?" Angelica asked with wide eyes.

"Yes, and then they were pulled into a spiritual, dream-like world that had been created through demonic intervention," the saint said solemnly. "I believe we must fight this battle by reaching their hearts, not through their reason, but through the gift of the imagination."

"But aren't our imaginations solely within our own minds, separate from each other's?" Liam asked, bewildered. "Isn't that a barrier, in that the imagination must be confined to its own grounds?"

The saint nodded. "This is an exceptional case. It is through dark, powerful forces that this villain has succeeded in pulling his victims into a world of his own creation. However, Our Lord is the God of all. He is not limited in his domain, and thus he is permitting you to take the fight to the enemy, to enter into the spiritual, imaginative world this fiend has fashioned." The saint shook his head, visibly dismayed at the magnitude of the task.

"It will not be an easy feat," he continued, "for his is a distorted, vile creation, but through the power of your advocate, the Holy Spirit, you will have the use of your own imagination. With wisdom and creativity, you will have a chance to free his captives and obliterate this evil."

"Wait!" Joachim called out suddenly. "Can someone who uses small words explain what all this means?"

Christian bent down, donning the speech of a caveman. "We go into evil man's made-up, scary world and set people free from bad guy."

"Got it!" Joachim smiled confidently. His smile faded a few seconds later when the meaning of the words set in.

"Where is the entrance to his world?" Serena asked, pondering the saint's words. "How do you go into someone else's...thoughts?"

"There is a door, and I will lead you there myself."

"Will you stay with us?" she asked with pleading eyes.

"I will. But the time to enter has not yet arrived. You will need to further prepare yourselves."

"And will we get gifts?" Mary added excitedly. "Last time, we got gifts."

"Most assuredly. We will arm ourselves with many gifts before entering his world. For now, you must return to the castle and assist your aunts in whatever way you can. Your offering of service will spiritually strengthen you. In two days' time, we will see each other again at the home for the elderly."

"You'll be at my Aunt Sophia's residence?" Will asked, surprised. "Will people be able to see you?"

"Indeed," the saint replied. "However, I believe it would be best to leave my cardinal's cape behind."

"Yes," Joachim affirmed. "You don't want anyone to think you're a superhero."

CHAPTER 11

A strange smell greeted the children when they returned to the castle.

"Did Aunt Dot burn something?" Joachim asked, scrunching up his nose.

"That's not a burning smell," Mary replied. "That's some kind of chemical-type smell."

Just then, Aunt Dolly burst into the kitchen with what looked like dark red, drippy syrup on her head, black tar on her face, and cotton balls between her toes.

"AHHH!" Joachim cried out. "What are you?! Why is your head bleeding all over? Why is your face all muddy? This is SO WEIRD!!!"

"It's alright, Joa," Aunt Dolly assured him. "Don't be scared."

"But why do you look like... that?" he stammered, his eyes wide with concern.

"All of this is helping me look pretty," Aunt Dolly replied, gesturing to her face and head.

Joachim looked very confused. "It's not working," he stated. "I think you looked prettier before."

"Oh, you silly guy! I won't be keeping all this on forever. When I take it off, I'll look pretty," she laughed. "Sometimes, we ladies like to make ourselves look extra beautiful for our suitors, especially when they are obviously head-over-heels in love with us. We know that they will probably want to spend a good portion of their day gazing at the charming, gloriously dazzling, mind-blowingly gorgeous display before them."

"Please stop," Aunt Frankie commanded, as she walked into the room. "I just ate a pickle, and I'd like it to stay in my stomach." Aunt Dolly opened her mouth to protest, but Frankie quickly pressed her finger against her sister's mouth. "Not one more nauseating adjective out of your mouth. I mean it!"

"Oh, go easy on her," Aunt Dot said, as she entered the kitchen. "She's been a bonky, balloopy, lovey-dovey since she got those flowers from Dr. Kingsley."

Liam cleared his throat and held up two fingers, indicating that there were two made-up words in the sentence.

"Yinz are all just jealous!" Aunt Dolly insisted.

"Not to intentionally change the subject," Allora interrupted, "but we were wondering if you have any work you'd like us to do for you. Will's here too and he's offered to help out."

"Well, thank you," Aunt Dot said cheerfully. "If you don't

mind, I'd love some helpers to work on sweeping and dusting the great room at the north end of the castle. We also have some boxes to unpack and set up in that room."

"And perhaps a few of you can work on the garden shed," Aunt Frankie added. "I'd like to know what tools were left there, so we'll know if we need to purchase anything in town."

"Sounds good!" Christian said. "Maybe Liam, Mary, Angelica, and Serena can work in the great room, and Will, Joachim, Allora, and I can work in the shed."

Allora nodded in agreement and the aunts also seemed satisfied with the teams. Aunt Frankie led Christian and his group to the garden shed while Aunt Dot brought the others to the great room.

The great room was a huge sitting area. There were a few bookshelves lining the walls and a number of dark burgundy leather loveseats and cream-colored couches with paisley patterns. The walls were plastered with striped wallpaper from the ceiling down about a third of the way, where it was met by large wooden panels with rich floral designs. A huge painting of the Blessed Mother hung beside a decorative fireplace, which was happily situated at the center of the room.

"There are a lot of fireplaces in this place," Serena mused.

"Yes," Aunt Dot affirmed. "Each room, in fact, has its own fireplace. It was how people heated their homes before they had electricity. The castle was built in 1882, which means it's very, very old."

"Whoa," Serena replied, as she bent down to dust the

bottom section of the first bookshelf. "Are these books from 1882? They sure look like it."

She ran her fingers across the spine of the books, admiring the spectrum of rich colors.

"That's pretty incredible!" Aunt Dot cried. "These books were here when I was a child. It's a wonder the owners that followed my grandfather didn't remove them."

"Perhaps they appreciated the historical element," Liam couldn't help commenting. "These books are antiques. I'm sure they were considered fixtures."

Aunt Dot nodded. "Yes, I think you're right. It would have been a shame if they had removed them."

Liam used a knife to cut through the packing tape used to seal one of the boxes. He had a confused look on his face as he pulled out the first item.

"Um...where would you like me to put this?" He held up a rock that filled his hand. It was covered in moss and glitter. Upon the rock, a large ceramic bullfrog had been glued. The tongue of the creature was elongated in a swirl that rose about five inches above its head. On the tip of the tongue, a large wired butterfly had been mounted. Someone had painted the wings of the insect bright pink and orange with yet more glitter. Around the frog's feet, small globs of hot glue had been used to create mushrooms, painted and smeared with, as expected, more glitter.

"Oh dear," Aunt Dot sighed. "That grossidious croaker is your Aunt Dolly's creation."

"We should have guessed, from all the glitter," Angelica stated.

"Should I put it on the mantle?" Liam hesitantly asked.

"If your Aunt Frankie was in here, she'd tell you to put it by the river to scare off rabid animals, but your Aunt Dolly would be heartbroken."

She scanned the room, her tongue resting on her lower lip. "Let's put it at the top of that bookcase," she said at last.

After Liam managed to place the item atop the highest shelf, Aunt Dot inspected the display. She scrunched her nose and whispered, "Maybe we should tuck it behind a few books up there."

After fulfilling his aunt's wish, Liam went back to the box and sighed as he pulled out another strange object: a large vase in the shape of a banana. It was covered in small, quilted yellow squares of varying patterns. The fabric was stiff with some type of clear finish.

He held up the eyesore. "Another one of Aunt Dolly's creations?"

"Not at all!" Aunt Dot assured him. "That's my delicious-ly-ambitiously crafted masterpiece. It's both practical and fabutastical, don't you think?"

"I'm sure it looks really nice when it's filled with flowers," Serena offered.

"It really does," Aunt Dot agreed, as she took the vase from Liam and placed it on a small table beside one of the loveseats.

Angelica was sitting on the floor near the fireplace, carefully cleaning the relief sculptures that decorated the posts leading up to the mantle. "This reminds me of the fireplace that opened up to a secret passageway," she quietly mused.

"Grandma said that there are secret passageways in this place. Is that true?" Serena asked her aunt.

"Your grandmother said she found one when we were staying here as young girls, but she's always had a big imagination. She may have been confused."

"That's funny," Serena replied, "because she said she pulled down on a book that was called *Rosa Mystica* and..." She ran her finger along the bottom shelf of books, reading the titles. "Yes! It's actually here!"

"WHAT!?" Mary cried out. She had been washing the large window on the north wall. She dropped her cloth and ran to Serena. "PULL IT! PULL IT!"

Aunt Dot was uncharacteristically quiet as she approached the bookshelf. She slowly put on her glasses, which had been dangling on a chain around her neck.

"May I?" Serena asked timidly.

"Well..., I..., I suppose so," she mustered, looking a little uncertain.

Serena placed her hand on the top part of the red, leather-bound book. She pulled slowly, but firmly. With little effort, it tilted down sharply, like a well-oiled lever. She could make out the sound of clicking gears and clinking chains. The children looked around the room, wondering where the opening would appear.

"It's not the fireplace," Angelica said, disappointedly. "I thought it might be, 'cause I heard some strange noises over here."

Liam wiggled the bookshelf, but it was completely secure. "It's not here either."

Mary examined the book. "What does *Rosa Mystica* mean anyway?"

"It's one of the titles used for Our Lady," Liam replied. "It means Mystical Rose. Mystical means hidden and the rose, being considered the most beautiful flower, is a reference to Mary: the most beautiful woman created. The idea of a 'hidden rose' indicates that, unlike the saints and martyrs, Mary's body cannot be found on earth, or inside some tomb, but was taken up into heaven: hidden from our earthly eyes."

"Hmmm. Do you think that might be a clue?" Angelica said as she traced her fingers along the relief sculptures. "Maybe there's an image of a rose or something here that would indicate the entrance to the secret passageway."

Mary was scanning the walls. "Or maybe it's the image of the Mystical Rose herself," she said, as she fixed her eyes on the painting beside the fireplace.

Aunt Dot shook her head. "I remember cleaning the wooden panels behind that painting as a child. There's nothing there."

"Yes," Mary said, "but you didn't know about the book." She ran to the painting. "Liam, can you help me?" Liam joined her and they lifted the beautiful portrait off the wall, setting it to the side.

Angelica stood up and placed her hands on her hips. She frowned as she faced the rich brown surface. "Okay, where is it?"

"I'm sorry, my dear," Aunt Dot said. "But I told you there's nothing there."

The panels were a series of tall, rectangular sections, each framed with ornate, wooden borders. At each corner, there were squares with a flower accent piece.

"Look for the rose," Serena suggested.

Liam scanned the four corners of the panel that had been directly behind the painting.

"Here!" he cried excitedly. He crouched down and placed his hand on the large wooden rose, turning it as one would turn a doorknob. He heard a click and the groan of hidden hinges as the panel opened into the wall.

Aunt Dot stared in awe. "Well, that's an unexpecadoozy!"

CHAPTER 12

The garden shed was halfway up the hill, between the castle and the forest. It was a large, double-doored wooden structure. Chipping paint and a sagging roof made it clear that it had been there for many, many years.

Aunt Frankie pulled open both doors, unleashing a slightly musty smell and some flakes of paint, which descended like confetti on the concrete ramp where she stood. "This place could definitely use a cleaning," she said.

"Are there lots of cobwebs?" Allora asked hesitantly. She was not a fan of spiders.

"It looks like this shed was scarcely used. I would imagine the previous owners hired landscapers to cut the grass and care for the property," Aunt Frankie commented. "Most of these tools have been here since my grandfather owned the property...and yes, there are quite a few cobwebs. But we'll have this place cleaned up in no time."

She started rummaging through large bins of rusted ware, while Christian and Will pulled out the larger items, like an antique reel lawn mower and a large bicycle. Allora picked up a broom and offered to sweep out the shed, including the cobweb-covered walls, which was a huge offering considering her aversion to the little eight-legged creatures.

Joachim was given a lengthy, old hose and instructed to untangle it. He started out well, sitting on the grass and weaving the thin tubing in and out as he attempted to undo the knots, but then he got distracted.

A small frog leapt out of a tall patch of grass and onto the hose.

"Hey!" Joachim called out. "Wriggle McSquiggles! I missed you." The frog looked blankly at the boy before hopping away toward the forest behind.

"No, don't go!" Joachim insisted, as he stood and began to chase his little friend.

The frog jumped over the tangled brush at the edge of the forest and headed into the thick, treed area beyond. Joachim was intent on catching him, calling out, "Your home is by the river, not over there! You're going the wrong way!"

The others were hard at work and with the sounds of metal scrap being thrown into an old wheelbarrow, the boy's voice could scarcely be heard.

Joachim ventured further into the woods, keeping his eye on the agile amphibian. Deeper and deeper they went, through leafy patches of ivy and around great boulders and mossy logs. Joachim tripped over a thick root protruding from the ground, but quickly pulled himself up and continued the chase. Finally, Wriggle McSquiggles came to a full stop. Joachim crept forward ever so carefully, wincing each time he stepped on a twig. The frog seemed willing enough to let the boy catch up to him. Joachim held his breath and, in one quick motion, scooped up the critter. He smiled with satisfaction, but only for a moment, for when he raised his head to survey his surroundings, he realized that he was standing in front of a small, broken-down cabin.

"Where have you taken us, Wriggle McSquiggles?" He nervously scanned the eerie structure, his eyes jetting back and forth. It was warped from the push of overgrown trees and fallen branches. Dense, knotted vines that looked more like dehydrated snakes were threaded through the windows, among broken shards of glass. The door hung diagonally, dangling from a single hinge, threatening to fall at any moment. It creaked, gently moving back and forth at the slightest breeze. Joachim was grateful that the sun was still shining, for he knew that this was not a place anyone would want to be after nightfall.

"I think we should go," he told the frog. He turned to face the forest behind him. Nothing looked familiar. His stomach sank as he realized he couldn't remember which direction he had come from. And now every path before him looked the same somehow, and each was overwhelmingly uninviting. He

began to call out. "ALLORA? CHRISTIAN? AUNT FRANKIE? ANYONE?" The boy was soon overcome with a feeling of dread. He unwittingly loosened his grip on his friend, who readily wiggled out of his hands and headed in the direction of the cabin.

"NO! Don't go in there!" Joachim cried. But the frog was fast and within seconds had hopped over the hanging door and through the entryway.

"No, no, no, no, no, no, no," Joachim repeated rhythmically, in an attempt to calm himself. The last thing he wanted to do was venture into the scary shack, but he loved his little friend and didn't want him to be alone.

"Okay," he whispered. "I'll do it. I'll go." He took a deep breath and slowly stepped up onto the front porch. He was careful not to tread on any of the most rotted boards. He called out to Wriggle McSquiggles. "I'm coming, little buddy."

Once he made his way over the front door, he surveyed the space beyond. It was one large room. It was fairly bright, as a tree had grown through the thin planks of wooden flooring and had broken through the ceiling above. Burnt, tattered linen hung over the window. It looked as though there had been a fire at some point, although it must have been put out fairly quickly, as most of the contents of the room appeared to have only been slightly singed. There was a small, overturned table at the center of the room. Beside it, Joachim could make out the remnants of broken chairs. There were a couple of old, blackened mattresses on the floor. They were threadbare, with rips and holes through which rusted springs sprouted in several directions. There was also a pile of aged newspapers that had somehow escaped any damage from the fire. Joachim picked up a copy and saw that it was dated October 9, 1963. As he lifted another paper, he saw what looked like a child's toy. It was a small car carved out of wood, with tiny wheels attached to the base. Somehow, standing in the room and staring at the old toy made Joachim feel less afraid—and even more so, sad. Someone had lived here, and it looked as though they were very, very poor. He felt bad, for the walls were so thin and he could only imagine how cold the residents must have been during the winter months.

The rustling of papers drew his attention to a small desk at the other end of the room. Joachim caught sight of a tiny, webbed foot on an open, weathered book. "Hey," Joachim said. "There you are!" He walked over to the desk and chastised the small frog for all the trouble he had caused. Wriggle McSquiggles looked as apologetic as a frog could look, and surprised Joachim by working his way into the loose pocket of the boy's cargo shorts. Joachim laughed. "Does this mean you're going to be a good frog from now on?" The frog croaked, and Joachim took it as his pledge of obedience.

He looked down at the desk. The book on which the frog had been seated was filled with handwriting. The papers were slightly damp and yellowed with age, but as he turned the pages he found that many passages were perfectly legible. "Looks like somebody's diary," he told his little companion. "Let's take it with us—and maybe the little car toy too."

They exited the cabin and Joachim let out a sigh. He still had no idea which way he should go. He looked at Wriggle McSquiggles. "I don't suppose you know the way back to the castle." The frog croaked, but seemed content to stay in the boy's pocket.

Joachim started by walking in the direction he believed to be west. With the sun leading him, he forged a path through the trees. He saw a few branches that appeared to have been freshly broken and hoped that they were an indication that he had come through the section not long before. He saw the crescent of a large root, and guessed it might have been the one that had caused him to fall on his way in. The tree attached to the root caused him to pause for a moment. It was gigantic! It had fallen down, and its ripped, exposed roots cascaded and twisted into a strange shape: a throne. It looked vaguely familiar, and Joachim soon realized that he was holding his breath. There was something unsettling about the sight. Normally, upon seeing something so clearly inviting its discoverers to claim their kingship, he would have jumped into the throne. But something held him back.

"You are wise not to place yourself in the heart of the enemy's lair."

Joachim jumped at the sound of the voice. He spun around and was relieved to be looking into the blue eyes of a dear friend. Joachim hugged the saint, burying his face in his black cassock.

"I thought I was lost. I was really hoping I would be able to get back, but wasn't sure if I'd be able to find my way. Now I know I'll be fine, because you're here."

Tears poured out of his eyes, surprising Joachim. He wiped his face with the back of his hand and then smiled, slightly embarrassed at his reaction. "I guess I was more scared than I realized."

"You were attempting to be brave for your tiny green friend's sake," the saint said with smiling eyes.

Joachim laughed. "Yeah, I guess so."

He thought for a moment. "What did you say about that weird tree throne again?"

"You may not realize it yet, but this day you have unlocked a clue which will reveal the motivation and nature of your enemy. This very forest plays an important role in the story, and this rooted abomination," he said, gesturing toward the throne, "is not a natural creation, but a symbol of a dark, depraved allegiance made years ago by a desperate, impoverished soul."

Joachim's eyes widened. "Can you take me out of here now?"

"Yes, of course, my boy. You are not in danger here; nay, not in this dimension at any rate, but I do ask you to remember well what you have seen today. It will be of the utmost importance in the near future."

Joachim was confused but nodded his head.

St. John Henry led him through the forest until he could make out the silhouette of the east tower just above the trees. He could hear the voices of his siblings calling out his name.

"Better make haste," the saint urged Joachim. "Your siblings are most worried about you, and I am confident that your aunt is anxious that your tardiness will make for another cold supper."

Joachim smiled and hugged the saint one more time before running toward the castle, the mysterious diary and toy tucked carefully under his arm.

CHAPTER 13

The tunnel extending from the great room was dark and narrow. Liam was using the flashlight app on his phone to light the path ahead. They had invited Aunt Dot to join them, but she had quickly declined, insisting that dinner would not make itself and instructing them to finish up their exploration of the secret passageway with enough time to "worsh" their hands and be ready for dinner.

The three sisters held each other's hands, forming a line. The pathway was embedded in the framing separating the rooms.

"There must be other secret doors," Serena whispered, as she noted thin lines of light leading into other rooms.

"We'll check out those openings some other time," Liam whispered back. "I want to see how far this thing goes."

"Why are you whispering?" Angelica asked. "We're not

trying to hide from bad guys or something."

"Whispering just feels appropriate," Serena said firmly.

As they neared what appeared to be the end of the tunnel, they found a small staircase leading down to a door. It was made of metal and there was a padlock securing it.

"Do you think the aunts would mind if we smashed this?" Mary asked.

"I'd feel bad about breaking it," Liam sighed. "It wouldn't be right."

"Can we do something that uses your keen ability to think outside the box and solve difficult dilemmas through the power of your advanced intellect?" Serena asked, impressing herself with her elaborate use of big words. She knew her older brother worked well when given a little boost of confidence.

Liam smiled bashfully. "Well..." he said, observing the door, "maybe we could evaluate the hinges, or the frame, or..." His voice trailed off as he continued to consider his options.

Angelica, who was finding it difficult to wait for Liam's analytical processing, let out a loud huff. She crossed her arms and leaned back against the stone wall. Her head whacked a wall sconce that had a round oil reserve and a large wick. It was clearly an antique, but Angelica was still mad at it for making her head sore. She swatted it in retaliation. The sconce shifted sideways and at the sound of scraping rocks, Angelica felt the stone surface behind her give way, opening to an adjacent passageway. She quickly grabbed onto Mary, in an effort to stabilize herself. It didn't work, and both tumbled into the newly exposed tunnel. Angelica stood up, dusting off the back of her pants.

"Well. That's that," she stated. "I figured it out! You're welcome, Liam." She flashed her brother a cheeky smile.

Liam's frown declared his disapproval, but secretly he was relieved that he wouldn't have to work out a solution for the metal door. Mary, who would have been justified in being angry with her sister for causing her to fall, was surprisingly ecstatic.

"Oh, this is awesome! A secret passageway within a secret passageway! And it was so perfectly hidden. I couldn't even see the seams along the edges of the stonework. This is too good!"

The children all stepped through the opening, surveying the archaic-looking construct. Suddenly, there was a loud grinding noise and a brief crunch, as the large stone doorway clamped shut.

The children all looked at each other in shock, their faces lit only with the bluish light from Liam's device.

"So, that's probably not a good thing," Angelica submitted. "We should try to get this thing to open up again."

"Check the walls to see if there's another sconce or something," Liam commanded. The walls held unlit torches, but no amount of maneuvering the fixtures proved fruitful in opening the door. They pressed on the various stones lining the walls in the area but again found the effort to be in vain.

They stood back and sighed in defeat.

"Well, I guess we'll just have to follow the pathway and see if there's a way out on the other end," Mary said decidedly.

They started down the path. It looked very different from the one they had traveled before. The tunnel was made of arched stonework and the floor was quite beautiful: a layer of pebbles pressed together, many with flecks of gold and silver. Liam decided that his flashlight app alone would not suffice in lighting the tunnel and so indulged Angelica and Mary's request to light torches for themselves.

The group traveled slowly, finding it rather unnerving that the light from Liam's device and the torches failed to illuminate the dense darkness in the distance. They had no idea how far the tunnel went. There were a few twists and turns, and the children were aware that they had completely lost any sense of their bearings.

"Is there an end to this tunnel? Are we going to end up in France?" Angelica mused.

"I wish we could go back," Serena said softly.

"We've got this," Mary said, reassuringly. "Besides, aren't you at all curious to see where this thing goes?"

"Well, I don't want to be late for dinner," the girl replied.

The children forged on until, finally, they caught sight of an opening ahead. The space beyond was a rough, cave-like chamber, with a ceiling that rose at least fourteen feet. The air was moist, and a faint roar could be heard, but there was no indication of its source. The room contained two sets of deep, metal, rusted shelves sitting on opposite walls. Boxes and trunks filled the space. Most were open and empty, but two were locked tight, and the children couldn't help wondering what treasures might be hiding inside.

Liam inspected the latches and found that they easily slid to the side, revealing small panels with buttons and the same strange letters that he had found on the trunk in his room.

"This is very, very strange," he said shaking his head.

"We still don't know what those weird letters mean," Angelica said matter-of-factly. "We should work on figuring out a way to get out of here."

"Easy-peasy," Mary declared. "There's a light glow coming from up there." She pointed to an oval-shaped opening in the stone, about six inches from the ceiling.

"How are we going to get up there?" Serena asked.

"The shelves!" Angelica cried out. "We can try to push one of them over there and climb up."

"Yes," Liam concurred. "But they won't be tall enough on their own to reach the opening. We'll need to use some trunks and boxes to build a platform high enough to make it up the hole."

It took all the children's strength to push the heavy shelves to the far wall. Angelica and Mary scrambled up to the top shelf and, with great effort, Liam and Serena lifted the boxes and trunks, one by one. Finally, the structure was complete.

"I'll go first," Angelica offered. She hoisted herself up through the opening and wiggled her way into a tiny tunnel. "Looks like we'll have to army-crawl our way through here," she called back to the others. "And we won't need the torches. In fact, Liam, you'll need to find a way to waterproof your phone."

"What!?" Mary cried. "What exactly is up there?"

"I'm not gonna lie: there may be a little swimming involved!"

"Oh dear," Liam said under his breath. He reached into his pocket and pulled out a plastic sandwich bag.

Mary stared at her brother. "You just happen to have that on you?"

"I always keep a plastic bag on me in case I find a curious specimen I'd like to take home to analyze," he said defensively. "That's a perfectly reasonable thing to do. I keep a lighter too. I like to be prepared."

"Well, at least your phone will be protected," she admitted.

The siblings all mounted the structure and, one by one, made their way into the tunnel. They wriggled their bodies, moving slowly along the path until the tunnel dipped down sharply, where it was fully submerged in cool water. From the brightness of the opening, Angelica concluded that the water couldn't be too deep—and she was right, for when she dove through the opening, swimming fervently, she surfaced within seconds. Bursting out of the water, Angelica smiled joyfully, for she found herself a few feet from the edge of the river, surrounded by beautiful, lush trees. She was about thirty feet from the top of the falls, and the sound of gurgling water and chirping birds left her feeling refreshed. The current was gentle, and Angelica wanted nothing more than to lift her feet and allow it to carry her over the falls.

One by one, her siblings popped up beside her, each feeling both relief and exhilaration. The children splashed around, savoring the rushing sensation of the water and the warmth of sunshine.

Liam climbed out of the river and looked around the area. "Well, we're not too far from the castle. I think there's a stairway just over there."

"I don't need a stairway!" Angelica declared. "I'm jumping off the falls into the lagoon!!!"

Serena looked a little hesitant. "Liam, I think I'll come with you."

"Not me!" Mary cried out. "I'm with Angelica!"

And with that the two girls swam down the river. The water was quite shallow close to the edge of the falls. The sisters stood and held hands, counting down until they both screamed excitedly and jumped off the edge, splashing into the waters below.

When they emerged, they pulled themselves up, giggling and talking nonstop about the experience. They followed the path back to the castle, meeting Serena and Liam along the way.

They were all laughing, but stopped abruptly when they

were met by a gasping Aunt Dot, who stared, mouth gaping, at the group of fully clothed, dripping children. She let out a stunned whisper: "It's dinner time."

Angelica couldn't help herself. "Well, we're all worshed up."

CHAPTER 14

Christian, Allora, Will, and Joachim were already seated at the dining room table, when the others walked in. Their jaws dropped as several squishy, splotchy wet shoes trudged across the floor. Angelica swept aside the wet, darkened hair that was plastered against her forehead.

"Hey!" she said with a goofy smile, loving their confused expressions. "So, we discovered (and got trapped in) a secret passageway within a secret passageway that led us to a hidden cave with mysterious locked trunks with the same strange letters as the ones we found in the boys' room, where we managed to build a tower up to the ceiling and squeeze through a tiny tunnel that brought us to the middle of the river." She smiled proudly.

"Oh, and we jumped down the falls!" Mary couldn't help adding. "So, how was *your* afternoon?'

Joachim piped up. "I was lost in the forest, and Wriggle McSquiggles led me into a freaky cabin, where I found a strange old diary and a toy car, then I tried to find my way here, but instead found an evil throne made of tree roots and Saint John Henry Newman appeared out of nowhere and showed me the way back to the castle."

Angelica's eyes widened. "Okay, so we all had eventful afternoons. It's not like it's a competition or anything."

"Now I'm starving!" Joachim added.

A voice was heard from the kitchen. "Music to my ears!" Aunt Dot walked in, carrying a large tray of corn on the cob. "Will Stevenson, you are staying for dinner," she stated. It was not a request, and Will was happy to obey her command.

Aunt Frankie entered the room, eyeing the corn. Aunt Dot raised her eyebrows. "See?" she sang. "I serve vegetables."

"Technically, they're grains or perhaps even fruit," she replied tenaciously.

"Oh, you!" Aunt Dot shot back. "Someday you're going to wake up and find Dolly's ugly croaker-butterfly rock sitting next to you."

Aunt Frankie scrunched up her face in disgust. "You wouldn't. UGH! The glitter would get into every crevice of every one of my possessions."

"You'd probably have a few little, sparkly specks under your eyes for weeks following the frog's visit. Your face would be scratched up from your feebly-weebly attempts to get them off." Aunt Dot lifted her nose into the air and eyed her

sister, threatening, "So, just try me."

And with that, she boss-walked back to the kitchen for the next dish.

Almost as soon as she left, Aunt Dolly flew into the room. She had an old, floral towel wrapped around her head. When she ripped it off, Aunt Frankie gasped. Her hair was a wild, mangled, bright red rat's nest. Layers of wiry, singed hair of varying lengths were clumped together in strange, warped curls.

"AHHH!" Joachim cried. "It still didn't work!!!"

Aunt Dolly shook her head, sighing mournfully. "I know, I know," she said. "Apparently, it's a bad idea to watch an enthralling romance movie while curling your freshly-dyed hair with a finicky curling iron. I burned off two big chunks of hair."

"Why did you keep trying to curl your hair after you burnt off the first chunk?" Aunt Frankie exclaimed, completely flabbergasted. "What were you thinking?"

"It was a really touching scene," Dolly protested. "So, I got distracted. Sue me for being a sensitive human being!"

Serena hurried to hug her aunt. "It's okay, Aunt Dolly," she said softly. "I'm sure you can find a way to style your hair and make it look really nice. It's a beautiful shade of red."

"Yes," Aunt Frankie said. "It's just like Ronald McDonald's."

Aunt Dolly shot her sister a look of defiance. "Just wait until I fix it up. You might even end up being a little jealous."

"No. I'm pretty sure I'd prefer a purple mullet to whatever you might do with that hair."

Ever the optimist, Aunt Dolly sat down with the children and smiled confidently. "It's going to be sensational. It's too bad you're not a trend-setter like me. I guess I'm the lone wolf of creativity in a dreary, hostile pack." And with that she stuck a full cob into her mouth, holding it only with her teeth, and growled at her sister.

"Did you say your prayers?"

Aunt Dolly promptly dropped the cob back onto her plate. "No, sorry," she whispered.

The rest of dinnertime was uneventful. As much as the aunts harassed one another, it was clear that they enjoyed being in each other's presence. They laughed, teased, and shared stories of their younger days. The children could tell that the sisters loved each other deeply and, perhaps, secretly enjoyed the constant drama.

Will loved the spectacle. It was a bit of comic relief, offsetting the weight of all he had witnessed in the past couple of days.

Allora leaned over and whispered, "I want to show you something I read in the diary that Joachim found in the cabin."

"Uh-oh!" Aunt Dot called out. "No whispering sweet nothings at the table," she teased.

Allora winced as her cheeks grew red.

"Well," Will offered, "I think we're all tempted to whisper sweet nothings about how amazing this meal is." Now Aunt Dot's cheeks were getting red. She beamed with pride.

"No, just no," Aunt Frankie said curtly. "That line was as cheesy as her stringed bean casserole."

Everyone laughed, except for Joachim, who sighed dreamily.

"I really, really love cheese."

That night, the children were able to video call their parents and their younger siblings. Kiara asked them to bring her a present when they returned home. Her face filled the screen on Liam's phone.

"I think the present should be a new watch," Kiara insisted.

"What happened to your old watch?" Allora asked.

"I dunno," the little girl replied with a baffled look. "I guess it just lost track of time."

The children giggled and assured her they would see what they could do.

They weren't quite sure what to tell their parents. Where would they even begin? They knew they would probably understand, as they had once been recruited to go on a mission themselves, but they also didn't want to worry them.

In the end, they decided to keep it simple.

"We found a key," Christian stated.

"And a cave," Liam said.

"And a door," Serena added.

"And a saint," Joachim said.

"And a mission," Allora joined in.

"And Grandma's secret passageway...but then another secret passageway," Angelica declared.

"And Aunt Dolly's glittery, bullfrog statue thingy on a rock," Mary added, scrunching up her nose. "It was really disturbing."

"Oh dear," their mother replied, "to all of it!" She sighed and glanced sideways, locking eyes with her husband. "Do you need help?" he asked the children.

"Yes," Allora admitted. "We've been assured that God will take care of us, but I know we'll need lots and lots of prayers."

"You can always count on us for that," their mother assured them.

Their father nodded reassuringly. "And if you need

anything else at any point, just let us know and we'll be there," he added.

Then he asked them all if they wanted to pray the Rosary and their night prayers together. The children were appreciative of the familiarity and warmth of the prayers, most of which were interrupted by little squeals and the sing-song voices of the youngest siblings. There was something so comforting about the experience: bathed in the love and support of their family, knowing they were all being held in God's hands.

CHAPTER 15

The next day, after a morning of cleaning, unpacking, sorting, and refereeing (Aunt Dolly and Aunt Frankie), the children offered to wash the windows in the boys' tower.

Christian, Joachim, and the girls got to work immediately; Liam, however, knelt in front of the trunk in their room. He grabbed a pad of paper with one hand, while his other hand held a pencil, which he tapped rhythmically against his tightly pressed lips. He was frowning, deep in thought, as he examined the line of buttons.

"Liam, what are you doing?" Christian asked.

"I'm sorry, it's just that I can't stop thinking about the letters," he said. "What's making it exceedingly vexatious is that I know the answer should be entirely within my grasp, and yet is somehow completely eluding me."

"Maybe it's just not the right time yet," Christian

suggested, as he rubbed one of the small windows with his cloth.

"Perhaps."

"I don't think I want you to find the answer," Joachim admitted. "That thing tased me, so I don't trust it."

"Maybe it was just trying to get our attention," Serena said with a shrug.

Liam lifted his pad of paper close to his face and began scribbling.

"What are you writing?" Angelica inquired.

Liam pointed to the letters one by one.

"This first letter is like our letter *S*; it's *sigma.* The next letter is similar to our *U* or *Y* and is called *upsilon.* It's followed by the letter that looks like our *X* but is actually our *CH* sound. It's called *chi.* Then we have the letter that looks like our *O* but is *theta*, representing the *TH* sound. Lastly, we have this letter: *iota.* It's the letter *I* in both languages."

"Whoa," Joachim said, looking very impressed. "You're a smart guy, Liam."

"I'm not feeling that smart right now, because I feel like I should know what this means and, ultimately, the proper arrangement of the letters."

"Well, we should really finish up the windows before Aunt Dot calls us for lunch," Allora advised. "Liam, it might be a good idea to take a break from the letters and come back to them later."

"Perhaps," he conceded.

"The windows are almost done," Christian stated.

"Good!" Allora said eagerly. "Then we have some time to look through the diary Joachim found."

She bounced onto the bed and carefully pulled out the small book.

"I read something in here that's a little freaky," she said.

"Shouldn't we wait until Will's here?" Mary asked.

"Aunt Dot invited him for lunch. I think she appreciates his appreciation of her cooking," Serena said with a little giggle.

"I hate waiting!" Angelica protested. "I think we can all agree that the amount of suspense and mystery contained in those pages is too much for anyone to bear."

"We can always catch Will up to speed later," Mary added, caught up in the excitement.

"Fine," Allora said. She had also been finding the wait to be nearly unbearable. She opened the book and squinted as she tried to make out the writing inside the front cover. "I think this is where the name of the owner of the diary was written, but there is some fire damage and it's gone. I can make out the date though: January 6, 1963."

She turned a few pages and then cleared her throat, as she began to read:

"January 6, 1963

I cannot tolerate this anymore. The obstinate fool is entirely to blame. He sits there, poring over his notes, while we freeze. Mother has been collecting paper. She has surmised that stuffing our clothing with the shredded fibers will somehow prevent the frostbite from penetrating our bones. I wish she would scream at him, wake the ridiculous mumblecrust from his determined path leading us to our ruin.

We once had such a fine life. Never in my wildest imaginings could I have foreseen such a descent into filth, waste, and hunger. We should have stayed in our last flat, even with the rat-infestation. There, at least we could leave a light on to scare the vermin away; here the feeble light from our pathetic wood stove does nothing to hold back the frigid daggers that easily pass through the paper-thin walls. I know I am not being a dutiful son by detailing the level of my disgust, but I stand by my words: I loathe the flesh from which I came. Here he stands: the pale, thin scobberlotcher who would rather leave our future to chance than try to find gainful employment that would pull his family from the gutter. He is adamant that this is a very temporary situation, but I know his words are never to be trusted."

The children stared at each other in disbelief.

"That is one seriously angry child," Mary said. "I mean, it's really sad that they were so poor, but he has such hatred for his father. It breaks my heart."

"He doesn't sound like a child. I wonder how old he is," Serena pondered.

Allora flipped through more pages.

"Here," she said. She read aloud:

"April 21, 1963

It's my birthday today. I can scarcely believe I've made it to 15. This winter has been as harsh and unrelenting as my father's laziness and stubbornness. My mother gave me a gift she made. It's a car she carved out of wood. She told me it represents the real car that she wants to give me someday. I laughed in her face. I know she meant well, and I felt a slight pang of guilt, but I am all too aware that the old man has dug us into a hole so deep that we will never be able to pull ourselves out. We are barely able to ensure we will continue to be fed and kept alive. We will never survive another winter here.

Since I was a young child, I shaped my mind with Shakespeare, Freud, Plato, and Socrates, hoping that through education, I might find a way to crawl out of this hole, but it has only made me further resent my state, for I realize that I am trapped in an impoverished life that rivals that found in a Dickens novel. There is no hope. Happy birthday to me."

"This feels really dark and depressing," Mary said sadly. "I feel so bad for the whole family."

"Read more!" Angelica insisted.

"There's a whole chunk of pages that are too rotted to make out," Allora said.

She leafed through until she came to the next legible section.

"July 4, 1963

It is the Fourth of July, and I am loath to hear the fireworks. They mock my pain, as they summon images of families carelessly lounging about, indulging in their gluttonous prosperity. I know it's self-torture, but I spied on the occupants of the castle again today. They were swimming, laughing, and eating copious amounts of food from their picnic tables-of-plenty. I saw the chubby, little red-haired girl again. She was eating more ice cream than her cone was meant to hold. I think she may have seen me, or perhaps she was simply waving her sparkler in my direction. Either way, she seemed to be a perfect representation of the 'haves' flaunting their goods in the face of the 'have nots.'

Someday, I will be the King of the castle. I will have an abundance of wealth. I will burn down this stupid shack and with it any evidence of the pathetic life to which I was subjected."

"Okaaaaay," Angelica said, looking very disturbed. "So, we're getting a lot darker."

"It gets even darker than that," Allora warned. "I read this really scary part yesterday. It's the one I was trying to show to Will before Aunt Dot made it awkward."

She turned to another section in the book and took a deep breath before reading aloud:

"September 16, 1963

It seems my luck is finally about to change. I went to the great fallen tree again. I can't believe that I was so afraid of the voices when I first heard them calling to me, when their intentions are so perfectly aligned with my own. They are my allies. They have the ability to permanently alter my fate. I understand now that perhaps it was I who summoned them.

They were the response to my earnest cry to the universe, demanding that I be given what is due one who has suffered tremendously. I can feel their strength, and therefore have willingly handed my soul over to them in exchange for great success, wealth, and power. It was an easy exchange, for I have been raised by a soulless father, so doesn't it follow that the son too may readily hand over his soul, especially if (in my case at any rate) it will mean the promise of all for which I have yearned?

The whole experience was euphoric. I questioned whether I had my wits about me, for how could I be engaging with the spiritual world? And so, they presented me with a gift: a symbol of our covenant. Almost as soon as I promised them my soul, the roots became animated, twisting into the shape of a throne. I am beside myself! Is it not the perfect foreshadowing of what's to come? My reign!"

"Oh wow," Mary said shaking her head. "So not good. I'm scared to ask if there's more."

"There is," Allora said sadly. "Another passage is completely intact... and completely disturbing."

She flipped to the last entry:

"October 30, 1963

The voices have made it clear that tonight is the night. I will try to remember all of their instructions. They have made it clear that it will take many years to lay the foundation, but I will soon rise in prestige and comfort, and one day, I will be the master of these lands. They have advised me of the necessity of proceeding slowly and carefully. I must be cunning, clever, and methodical if I am to achieve my goal.

But tonight, oh tonight, I will watch my old life, the insult that is my past, go up in flames. It will be exhilarating! I am going to ignite the biggest fire and burn everything! Not even you, Dear Diary, will survive the blaze. Tonight I leave the old world behind and someday will return, as King."

Allora slowly closed the book, and the children stared at

one another in silence.

"YODEL YODEL OLEY OLAH LAY HEE HOO!!!"

The children jumped at the sound.

"It's okay," Angelica called out to her aunt. "We're not in our *haynies*!"

"Lunch time!" Aunt Dot called up from the spiral staircase.

"Coming!" They all called out at once.

CHAPTER 16

Aunt Dot grabbed a large tray from the cupboard, humming as she turned to collect the series of plates filled with roasted garlic, baby potatoes and pan-fried fish.

She carried the tray confidently, turning her backside to the door leading to the dining room and pushing it open.

The door swung easily, banging into the wall behind.

"You are all in for such a treat, if I do say so myself!" she declared to the children. "It's fish!"

Upon her entry, she noticed the children talking quietly, but they quickly hushed each other as she placed the tray on the table. Will was seated beside Allora. He looked highly disturbed.

"My, my, my," Aunt Dot mused. "If I were a neddy-Nel-lie, I'd be tickling arm-pitlings to find out what yinz were all whispering about, especially since it has Will looking as pale as a frozen pierogi!"

Mary snorted.

"Joachim found a broken-down cabin yesterday in the back woods. Do you know who lived there?" Allora asked.

Aunt Dot seemed surprised. "Hmmm, you know, I really don't. I think that was built around the same time as the castle. It was a bunkhouse for the lumberjacks who worked the area, but I believe they moved on to a new site shortly after their work began, and the cabin was abandoned. I never actually saw the bunkhouse, as our grandfather wouldn't let us go too far into the woods." She eyed Joachim. "I don't think *anyone* should venture that far into the woods."

"I didn't mean to," Joachim said in his defense. "I was following my pet frog."

"I do seem to recall that there was a fire there years ago. My grandfather said that he could see the smoke from one of the upper rooms of the castle. It didn't last long though. He said that he had rung the fire department, but by the time they arrived the fire was already out."

"Was anyone hurt in the fire?" Serena asked.

"I don't believe so."

"And no one knows what caused the fire?" Christian asked.

"I don't think there was much of an investigation, as it was already pretty run-down. No one was supposed to have been living there. In the end, I believe everyone assumed that the fire had probably been caused by lightning." Aunt Dot glanced at the table. "Sakes alive! The fish is getting cold! Come on, let's say our prayers and dig in."

Will didn't have much of an appetite. The dark nature of the mysterious author of the diary left his stomach feeling a little queasy. He had an eerie feeling that the boy from the cabin and the terrible things that were happening at the seniors' residence were somehow connected.

Aunt Dolly sashayed into the room. She looked like she was making her way down a runway: pausing, posing duck-faced with her hands on her hips before changing directions, spinning and freezing with her chin lifted in the air.

"So?" she sang out. "What do you think?"

Joachim raised his hand, as though he were in a classroom.

Aunt Dolly pointed to him, and he smiled and blurted out, "Your hair's not ugly anymore!"

Aunt Dolly was a little taken aback, but then smiled and cried out, "YES! My hair is sensational once more!" Her hair did look so much better. It was a lot shorter than before, but admittedly very stylish.

"And the best part is," she continued, "my boyfriend is coming over to see me today, and he is going to, legit, lose it when he sees how youthful I look with my new 'do!"

Her excitement was contagious and the children were happy to partake of her joy. It was a welcome relief after exposure to the dark musings contained in the diary.

"Liam, finish your fish," Aunt Dot insisted as she observed his plate.

"Sorry, Aunt Dot," he replied. "My mind is a little preoccupied with a puzzle I've been trying to solve."

"Oh, I love puzzles!" she exclaimed. "But I also love fish."

"Fish," he whispered.

"Yes," she replied, smiling, but also looking slightly confused.

"FISH!" Liam exclaimed excitedly. "FISH! AMAZING! How could I not have realized it?!"

Everyone sat silently, exchanging looks that seemed to question the boy's sanity.

"Guys!" he said, smiling. "It's fish!"

He suddenly jumped up from the table and darted toward the stairs.

The other children ran after him. Serena turned back as she ran, calling out, "Sorry, Aunt Dot. We'll be right back to finish up and help with dishes!"

Aunt Dot sat, shaking her head, mumbling, "I just don't understand. I told him it was fish right at the beginning of the meal."

The children ran up the stairs and congregated in the boys' tower, forming a semi-circle around the trunk.

Will examined the panel. "Are these the strange letters you guys mentioned yesterday? The ones that match the ones on the trunks you found in the cave?"

"Yes," Allora answered. "Liam's been trying to figure out the right configuration."

"It's fish," he said again, smiling. "Have you ever noticed

cars that have a fish ornament or bumper sticker on the back?"

"Yes," Will answered. "It's a Christian symbol."

"That's right," Liam affirmed. "It is an ancient Christian symbol. The early Christians created it when they were being persecuted by the Romans. They used the Greek word for fish as an acronym for who they knew Jesus to be. The letters on the trunk are scrambled, but here is the correct order." He pointed to each letter as he spoke. "This letter that looks like *I* should be pressed first. It stands for *Jesus*. Next is the *X*, which is the *CH* for *Christ*, followed by the one that looks like an *O*, which stands for *God's*, and the *Y*, which is *Son*. Lastly, we have the letter that kind of looks like a backwards three, and it stands for *Savior*."

He pressed each button as he repeated the words. "Jesus, Christ, God's Son, Savior."

After the last button had been pushed, the whole trunk began to glow and vibrate. The children took a step back as the lid shot open with a great red flash of light.

Christian was the first to creep forward and peer over the lip of the chest.

"What are those?" he said, awestruck.

The others approached, timidly peeking into the trunk. The metal box was lined in beautiful, white satin. It contained eight balls of red flames. They were burning brilliantly, but the satin remained unaffected.

"Do you think we can touch them?" Joachim asked his older siblings.

"Let's try it!" Christian cried out, impulsively thrusting his hand into the chest.

"Christian!" Allora exclaimed, annoyed at her brother's gumption. "Why do you always do stuff like that?"

"I don't know," he admitted. "But look! This is so cool!" He slowly lifted his hand out of the trunk, revealing one of the masses of flame in the palm of his hand. "It's not burning me," he assured the others. "You should each take one."

One by one, the children reached in and pulled out a ball of flame. Serena giggled, for the flickering of the flames tickled her hand. It was warm and sent a comforting vibration through her fingers.

Each child stood staring at the miraculous, enchanting form in their hands. They were filled with a sense of reverence and wonder. Suddenly, each ball began to change.

Liam's was first. The flames swayed and danced, turning into a small flaming dove. It flew passionately just above his open palm, swirling and curling, leaving a trail of glowing light behind its tiny tail feathers. The trail formed cursive letters. As the dove disappeared, a floating, luminescent word remained: Wisdom.

It hung in the air before stretching out into an enthralling ribbon of light, which dove back down into Liam's hand, swirling rapidly just inside his palm. Faster and faster it spun until it seemed to solidify into a rather ordinary looking object: a circular pendant that resembled the top part of a magnifying glass. It was attached to a thick chain.

"Interesting," Liam murmured. "It's a monocle."

Next, Allora's flame was on the move. Again, they witnessed the formation of a dove, and through its fervent flight it fashioned another word which lingered in the air: Understanding.

Once more, the word stretched out and flew down into Allora's palm. It twirled at a great speed, until it became a blur of light, which then transformed into a solid, metallic object: a locket. It was gold and fixed to an intricate chain.

"Beautiful," she whispered, as she carefully placed it around her neck.

Next, Joachim's flame transformed into the word Counsel, and the object he found in his hand was a compass. It too hung from a long chain. "So cool," he said with a big smile. "Now I won't get lost again."

After Joachim, Angelica's flame was activated. The word that hung above her hand was Fortitude .

The object that appeared in her palm was a small, smooth rock secured to a silver chain. At first, she looked a little disappointed, thinking it a rather plain object compared to her siblings', but then she noticed that it could detach from the chain, as though it were magnetized.

"Hmmm," she thought aloud, "very interesting. I can't wait to find out what this thing can do."

Mary's flame was now beginning its dance. Her word was Knowledge, and the object was a pair of gloves. They were short but elegant, made of very fine, iridescent chainmail.

They were surprisingly stretchy, and perfectly snug when she tried them on.

"Oooh," Mary cooed. "Love them! I was kind of hoping for a necklace too, but these are so cool."

Serena's flame then began its transformation. The dove's trail created the word Piety, and Serena was elated to find a necklace with a large, ruby-red heart-shaped gem laying in her palm. She gingerly examined the pendant, whispering, "How pretty."

Next, Christian's flame began to swirl, unleashing the dove. Above his hand, it was not one word that appeared, but four: Fear of the Lord. The words formed four long ribbons of light. Christian watched, completely entranced, as the ribbons remained in the air, thickening, lengthening and then folding into each other, weaving and braiding until they had become a long, sleek, golden rope. The rope slowly coiled before draping itself over Christian's extended hand.

Christian gripped the cord and smiled as he secured it to his side, using his belt. He nodded, as though very satisfied with the item.

Everyone looked at Will, whose flame remained a constant ball, still sitting within his palm.

"Curious," Liam mused.

"What?" Allora asked her brother.

"Well, it's apparent that we have each been given a gift of the Holy Spirit," he answered. "Of course, we all have access to all these gifts, especially through the Sacrament of

Confirmation, but it seems as though we are each being called to focus on a particular gift, one that I'm sure is meant to assist us in our particular role in this mission. However, there are seven gifts of the Holy Spirit, and there are eight of us here. So, I'm wondering what gift Will is holding in his hand."

It was as though the fire heard him, for it began to grow and swirl into a dove, seemingly in response to his words.

Will awaited in anticipation as the dove vigorously formed a sentence: Heart speaks to heart.

The words began their swirling descent, and Will soon found a golden crest, about the size of large coin, in the palm of his hand. Three red hearts were engraved on the object, two at the top and one at the bottom, separated by a thick, red, zigzagging line.

Liam approached him, adjusting his glasses as he gazed at the object with great interest.

"Huh! Very appropriate," he said. "That's Saint John Henry Newman's crest. It can be seen on his coat of arms, which contains the Latin phrase: *Cor ad cor loquitur.*"

Liam excitedly reached into Will's hand but stopped short, remembering himself. "Oh, I'm sorry. Do you mind?" he asked.

Will was happy to comply, wanting to learn as much as possible about his gift. "Not at all," he said. "Go ahead."

Liam flipped the object over. "Ah, here it is, the very phrase inscribed on the back of the crest. The translation was already revealed by the fiery dove: *Heart speaks to heart.*

It was Newman's motto. So, it seems your gift is connected in a special way to our friendly neighborhood saint."

Will smiled, touched by the distinctive gift.

"I think we'll need to check in with St. John Henry to learn more about all the gifts," Liam added. "These are some really interesting manifestations. I'm eager to learn how to use them."

Their time of exhilaration and enthrallment was interrupted by an excited, ear-shattering shrill.

Angelica raised an eyebrow. "I'm thinking that siren is indicating that Aunt Dolly's 'boyfriend' has arrived.

"But isn't she all the way down on the first floor—like two full staircases and about five rooms away?" Will asked incredulously.

"Yup," Allora answered. "We should be very grateful we weren't in the same room when she let that out."

They all heartedly agreed, and then tucked their gifts away, before heading down to join the aunts.

CHAPTER 17

Aunt Dolly quickly checked herself in the large mirror over the fireplace. She had it all planned out. She planted herself on the staircase, hoping to gracefully and romantically descend the steps just as Frankie, having answered the door, would be showing Dr. Kingsley into the hallway. She pinched her cheeks as she practiced a few different versions of potential greetings. "Dr. Kingsley, you are such a dear for visiting little old me," she said, draping herself over a rail. "No, that won't do," she said, straightening up as she cleared her throat and tried again. "Kingsley, I can't tell you how long I've waited for this day...no!" She snapped her finger in frustration. "Too forward." She tried one more time. "Why Kingsley, I had almost forgotten you were coming over today." She threw back her head dramatically and swung around the post of the railing. "I've had so many men vying for my

attention lately that it must have slipped my mind. But maybe, if you speak to me with that sweet little accent of yours, I just might allow you to sweep me off my…" There was a cough. Aunt Dolly turned her attention to the two people standing just behind her, at the bottom of the stairs.

Aunt Frankie did not look impressed, as she stood with her arms crossed over her chest. Beside her stood a somewhat confused Dr. Kingsley. Aunt Dolly's cheeks turned as red as her hair. A strange, wide-eyed, frozen expression was glued to her face. She could barely move her lips as she whimpered, "Oh, hello."

"Hello, Dolly. You look beautiful," the polite gentleman offered. "Did you do something to your hair?"

Dolly's face immediately transformed into a big, beaming smile. "Oh, YOU!" she cried out, touching her hair and pursing her lips. "Maybe just a little trim."

"Well," Frankie interjected, "it seems *that sweet little accent of yours* did the trick after all."

She let out an annoyed huff and briskly left the room calling out, "Once you're done *sweeping her off her feet*, I'm sure she'll be happy to give you a tour of the place."

The children descended the staircase and greeted the doctor.

"Those are very pretty flowers," Serena said, gesturing to the beautiful bouquet he held in his hand.

"Dr. Kingsley!" Aunt Dolly cried out. "You shouldn't have!"

"A small token of my admiration," he replied. "And please, call me George."

"Oh, Georgie! Thank you!" Aunt Dolly exclaimed, batting her eyelashes. "Well, I think we should give you the grand tour."

"I would very much enjoy that," he said, his eyes taking in the beauty of the intricate, ornate wooden accents on the staircase.

Aunt Dolly led the way, threading her arm around

Dr. Kingsley's. She swayed her hips as she motioned to the various rooms and works of art lining the walls in the hallway. When they came to the great room, Kingsley seemed quite intrigued.

"This is exquisite," he said, admiring the rich decor. His eye caught sight of the strange banana vase, and Angelica giggled when she noticed his abrupt wince. He recovered quickly and, once more, his face bore a pleasant smile.

"I want to show you something!" Aunt Dolly told her guest, excitedly scanning the room. "Wait. Where is it? Where's my cute little froggy?"

Liam's eyes grew wide and he tried not to look in the direction of the hidden monstrosity.

"Oh well," she said, lightly shrugging, "I guess you can see it later....It would be an amazing wedding cake topper.... I mean, if someone ever needed something on top of their wedding cake....I mean, if someone were to be getting married in the near future...or, you know...."

There was an awkward silence as the children were yet again astonished at their aunt's unfiltered verbal outpouring, but Dr. Kingsley simply patted her arm and gave her a shy but encouraging smile.

He then unhooked his arm from his companion's (although it took a little effort to pry himself away from her grip), and walked over to inspect the bookcases more closely. He ran his hand across a few of the books halfway up the shelf, wiggling a few of them.

"These books appear to be incredibly old; many of them are first editions of classics. How splendid," he commented.

He then made his way over to the wood-paneled walls beside the fireplace, admiring their craftsmanship. He traced his finger over the wooden floral reliefs, before gently knocking on the smooth panels.

"This is such fine work," he said, his voice full of admiration. "Stunning workmanship, beautifully and solidly built. I hope you can pardon my enthusiasm, but I've always taken a keen interest in Victorian style and architecture, and this house..." he turned to look into Dolly's eyes, "holds unparalleled beauty."

Aunt Dolly blushed and let out a strange, schoolgirlish shrill.

"How many bedrooms are in the castle?" he inquired. "I would imagine there must be quite a few to allow you to accommodate your nieces and nephews."

"There are nine, and they're very large. The children are sharing the attic and the east tower. We thought they would enjoy the view and the unique charm of those rooms."

"There's a bedroom in the tower?" Dr. Kingsley said, his interest clearly piqued. "That must be an amazing sight. I would so enjoy seeing it, if you wouldn't consider it an imposition. Is there a view into the coned roof structure? I would love to inspect the architectural details."

"Yes, there is, and I'm sure the boys would be more than happy to show you their room."

Joachim nodded in agreement and led the way.

As they mounted the staircase, Dr. Kingsley continued to enthusiastically inspect the panels lining the wall. He gave another little knock on a panel beside an old painting of a regal-looking man. He stopped and inspected the small metal plate at the bottom of the frame.

"Lord William J. Mitchell, 1854–1940."

"That's the first owner of the castle," Aunt Dolly stated, hoping to impress Dr. Kingsley with her historical knowledge. "He had this place built for the love of his life when they immigrated from England. I think their only child was born that same year. Lord William's grandson took over the property after his death in 1940. Unfortunately, the grandson was into gambling, and in 1955, he lost the house to my grandfather in a single hand of cards!"

Kingsley stopped abruptly on the staircase, causing a few of the children to bump into their aunt who was directly behind him. Serena was grateful for her aunt's extra padding.

"You can't be serious!" the doctor cried out, clearly angered and appalled. He caught himself. "I apologize. Obviously that exchange worked out very well for your family, but I'm shocked that the lure of gambling would cause someone to willingly risk such a family treasure." He shook his head. "It's very sad...but I guess it does make for an interesting story."

"Yes, it does," Aunt Dolly affirmed, although her eyes were a little wide with surprise at her boyfriend's outburst. She then smiled as her optimism took over. *Hidden passion, how romantic*, she thought to herself, trying to stifle a giggle.

When the group entered the library, Dr. Kingsley let out a sigh of delight at the sight of the rounded walls, filled top to bottom with books. "This is quite impressive," he said to his companion. He walked over to a bookshelf, inspecting the titles of a series of books on the middle shelf. He pulled a few out halfway, reading the titles, before discovering a section where there appeared to be a group of works containing the family archives. "Is this where the history of the castle is written?" he asked.

"Well, it doesn't have the story about the infamous poker game, but it does have details about the family, the property and the construction process. Sadly, I haven't read most of those books. Although, of my sisters, I'm possibly known as the smartest little family bookworm."

"Really?" The voice came from an annoyed Aunt Frankie. Aunt Dot cleared her throat in a chastising manner. The two stood at the library's entrance, shaking their heads and glaring at their baby sister.

"I did say *possibly*, meaning it's open to debate."

Joachim turned excitedly to his two aunts. "Aunt Dolly told us that your grandfather won the castle in a hand of cards!"

Aunt Dot gasped. "Dolly! That's not something you should be telling the children!"

"Well it's true," she said crossing her arms and lifting up her chin.

The doctor walked over to the spiral staircase and placed his hand on the black rail. "Shall we?" he asked, looking up with an eager smile.

"Of course," Aunt Dolly affirmed.

"I'll lead the way!" Joachim called out as he scrambled past the doctor and up the stairs.

Dr. Kingsley followed quickly behind, mirroring the boy's enthusiasm. When everyone had mounted the steps, they found Kingsley standing over the metal trunk, peering down.

Angelica was soon at his side, examining the doctor's face.

"This is very intriguing. It looks like a treasure chest. I don't suppose you were able to open it?" he said with a wink.

"Um..." Angelica faltered. She wasn't sure if they should really be discussing the miraculous things they had witnessed just before, especially as they were linked their mission, and St. John Henry had not given them permission to disclose the details to anyone outside their group.

Allora interrupted, "How did you know it was locked?"

The doctor smiled. "Well, aren't treasure chests usually locked?"

"Yes, I guess that's true," she answered.

"That trunk is practically a fixture here. I remember it as a child, when we girls came up here to play. It's impossible to lift and I think it's likely welded shut. We tried almost everything to get it to open."

Christian looked up into the coned ceiling, gesturing to Dr. Kingsley. "So, what do you think of these architectural details?" he asked. But the doctor was not listening. He had found his way over to one of the small windows overlooking the forest. He stood silently, lost in thought. Aunt Dolly soon joined him, hooking her arm through his, and sighing sweetly. "Isn't it lovely, Georgie?" He placed his hand over hers, his expression relaying his appreciation of the majestic view. "Simply magnificent," he whispered. "What a glorious sight. And I must say, you crown it with your beauty."

Aunt Dolly sighed, swooning, her knees noodling. Dr. Kingsley had difficulty keeping his balance. Liam and Christian rushed to Aunt Dolly's side, stabilizing the lovestruck victim.

Angelica shook her head. "You have to be careful what you say, Dr. Kingsley," she advised. "She can only handle so much."

Aunt Dot urged the group to head back downstairs. "I've set us up with some tea and treats in the dining room," she said. The doctor suggested that the others start making their way down first. "If you don't mind, I'd like to just take one last look out these windows before joining you. I'll be sure to close the hatch," he offered.

"There isn't a hatch," Liam said, "or any kind of door for that matter. Aunt Dot yodels whenever she wants to come up."

The doctor laughed heartily. "Now that is something I would love to witness."

Angelica raised her eyebrows and whispered, "Be careful what you wish for."

The children and the aunts descended and then exited the library, except for Liam, who hung back hoping to scan the books for more information on the gifts of the Holy Spirit.

Dr. Kingsley swiftly descended the staircase, but instead of heading out, he lingered in the library, staring at the section containing the family archives. Liam approached the gentleman, who seemed startled by his presence.

"I'm sorry; I didn't mean to scare you," Liam said.

"Not at all," the man replied. "I'll admit, I wanted to have another look in the Mitchell family archives. I believe Lord William J. Mitchell commissioned the building of the Monterey Seniors' Home. He was on the board of directors for the last years of his life, and I believe he had some connection to the Keble family. Roger Keble is the current director, and between you and me, I believe something is amiss. I thought perhaps I could gather some information."

"Well I'm sure Aunt Dolly would be more than happy to have you visit again and spend some time going through the archives."

"Yes, I think that would be quite helpful."

"We should head down, though," the boy sighed. "If we take too long, you will definitely be exposed to Aunt Dot's yodeling."

Dr. Kingsley chuckled, and the two headed to the dining room.

The doctor spent the remainder of his visit offering his undivided attention to Aunt Dolly. She was fully smitten, and the children were convinced that if Kingsley asked her that very moment for her hand in marriage, she would be calling Fr. McCranager and booking the church for the following day. It was nice to see her so happy, caught up in her whirlwind romance, though Aunt Frankie continued to eye Dr. Kingsley suspiciously, keeping her wooden spoon within reach.

CHAPTER 18

The next morning the children again attended daily Mass with their aunts. Fr. McCranager seemed very happy to see them. He pulled them aside after Mass.

"You are a very good influence on your aunts," he assured the children. "They have been very well-behaved since your arrival."

Aunt Dot ushered the children to their van. "It's true," she whispered. "Dolly and Frankie have been on their best behavior, and I'm convinced it's the reason that Father's homilies have been less than ten minutes long."

She joined the children in the van. Aunt Dolly and Aunt Frankie were returning back to the castle with Christian. Aunt Frankie was expecting a package and wanted to be there for its arrival. Aunt Dolly was forced, against her will, to go back. In her enchanted, day-dreamy state, she had fed the chickens milk chocolate-covered raisins and their little, feathered bodies had rejected the food in a very messy manner.

"How could you have not realized that you were feeding them chocolate?!" Aunt Dot had exclaimed.

"I don't know," a very apologetic Aunt Dolly had wailed. "I had a secret stash of my goodies hidden in a chicken feed pail, and I guess I just got distracted and reached into the wrong section."

Aunt Frankie's eyes were bulging. "Why would you hide a stash of candy with the chicken feed?"

"I get hungry sometimes when I'm feeding them!" Aunt Dolly had thrown back. "So sue me for having an appetite!"

Aunt Dot was furious. "I'd like to sue you for almost killing the chickens!"

Aunt Dolly had burst into tears, and her sisters felt sorry for their little sister. They offered their forgiveness to the penitent chicken-offender, but it was decided that she would join them for Mass and then promptly return home. She would be manning a hose for the remainder of the morning, and tending to the poor chickens. Christian had offered to help. As he had a particular distaste for the task, he knew it would be a truly heroic offering.

He was also hoping to drop into the library and search the family archives. He had told Liam the night before about the conversation he had overheard between Pam and Dr. Kingsley at the seniors' home. He mentioned the doctor's suspicions about the director. Liam shared Kingsley's idea of checking the archives to see if there was a connection to Roger Keble, and Christian decided that it might be helpful for him to assist with the investigation.

In addition to his sleuthing, he knew that Aunt Dolly would most likely need a shoulder to cry on, after being deprived of a visit with the love of her life.

At the seniors' home, Aunt Dot and the children were met at the entrance by Pam and Will. Pam didn't look happy.

"Is it a bad day?" Allora asked softly. Will nodded, keeping his eyes fixed on the ground.

As they entered the facility, their spirits were lifted as they saw Adele ushering a tall, thin priest with knowing blue eyes. St. John Henry was dressed in his black cassock and when he caught sight of the children, he smiled warmly and winked.

Adele greeted the group. "Hello, everyone! This lovely man is Father John Henry. He's offered to visit with the residents today." She held her hand just at the side of her mouth, as though she were sharing a delicious secret. "He's such a gem!"

"I think everyone here knows that *you* are the gem," he laughed. "I am but an old soul hoping to reflect some of your light."

Pam stepped forward. "Father, would you come and see my sister and perhaps give her a blessing? She's not doing very well."

"Absolutely," the priest answered, his eyes conveying his genuine empathy.

Aunt Dot sighed. "Sophia's room is pretty small; would some of you be alright with joining me in the common room?"

"Actually, I'd really like that," Angelica replied. "I'd like to see Edward."

"And I'd like to hear Lillian play the piano again," Serena added.

"I'll come too," Liam said. He also enjoyed playing the piano. "Maybe we can play a duet."

Aunt Dot led half of the group to the common room, while Pam, Will, Allora, Mary, and the saint went to visit Sophia.

When they arrived at her room, they found Sophia sitting at the side of her bed. She was silently staring out the window.

"Sophia?" Pam said gently. "I've brought some visitors."

St. John Henry sat beside the woman and spoke softly to her.

"Hello, Sophia, I am delighted to meet you. I am all sorrow that you have so often been robbed of the presence of mind which allows you to connect with your family. Know that you are loved and that you will always be surrounded by those who see the beauty and dignity that defines you. Now, if you don't mind, I would love to offer you my blessing."

He lowered his head and began to utter an inaudible prayer. He raised his hand, just above her forehead, wincing slightly, as though he could feel her pain. Then, in a touching testament of unity, tears welled up in his eyes, and at the very same moment, Sophia's eyes also filled with tears. She remained in her frozen state, but the others were astounded by the obvious connection the old man had made.

Will was stiff with emotion, his back pressed against the wall. He appeared to be holding his breath, his lips tightly shut. When he relaxed slightly, his eyes became warm and watery.

Pam sniffled and ran a finger below her eyes to wipe her own tears.

"Thank you so much, Father," she whispered. "That was truly beautiful." She gestured to the door. "Could I get you some coffee or tea?"

"Tea would be lovely," the priest replied. "Perhaps we can go together, as I would love to check in with some of the other residents."

"Of course," she replied. As they exited the room, the saint turned back to the children and quietly pointed to the painting on the wall.

"The sketchbook," Mary whispered. "We should see if Sophia drew anything since we last visited."

Will remained fixed in his position.

Allora slowly approached the boy, gently placing her hand on his arm. "Are you okay?" she asked.

"Heart speaks to heart," he whispered. "I think I understand my gift. I could hear her heart speaking, and Saint John Henry Newman's too. She told him she that she can't

break free, and that somehow she was alright with that...that somehow, she believed it best to remain where she was." Will shook his head in confusion. "Then he told her that it was not God's will for her to remain a captive. He said that she was loved so much that God was sending us to help her find her way back home."

"The question is, who is actually the one holding her captive?" Mary said.

"Perhaps the answer to that is in the sketchbook," Allora said, as she approached the painting. She promptly lifted the frame from the wall and laid it face down on the bed beside Sophia. Will sat on the other side of his aunt, placing his arm around her shoulders. The book was still in its paper pocket and Allora easily slid it out. Mary placed the painting back on the wall and the children all gathered around the book, as Allora turned to the section that was just past the pages that had previously been ripped out.

"She did it," Allora whispered, enthralled by the images before her. "These drawings reveal everything."

CHAPTER 19

In the common room, Angelica sought out her friend Edward, but he wasn't there. She looked around hoping to find Adele, but instead found herself face-to-face—or rather face-to-clipboard—with the director.

She had been told about Dr. Kingsley's suspicions and so was hesitant to speak to the tall, broad-shouldered man in his tailored suit. However, she really wanted to know the whereabouts of her friend.

"Excuse me," she said, looking squarely into Keble's eyes. "I can't seem to find my friend. His name is Edward...I don't remember his last name, but his wife's name is Violet and she's in the east wing. Do you know where he is?"

The man frowned slightly and then lifted up a few pages attached to his clipboard, examining them.

"I'm sorry, young lady," he said, looking back to Angelica.

"It seems your friend is now also in the east wing."

"What?" she cried. "But he was fine just two days ago. Why is he in the east wing?"

"I'm sorry, but I'm really not at liberty to discuss his case, due to patient confidentiality."

"Can I see him? Is he allowed visitors?"

"Truly, I am sorry, my dear, but I don't think that's a good idea."

Just then, Kingsley entered the common room. "Is there a problem here?" he asked as he approached the two.

"Not at all," Keble said, glaring at the doctor. "I was just informing...sorry, what is your name dear?"

"Angelica."

"...Angelica, that it may not be a good idea for her to visit a patient in the east wing."

Dr. Kingsley eyed the man coldly. "She can come to the east wing if I accompany her."

Keble shook his head, disagreeing with the suggestion. "You probably have patients to attend to. If you feel it appropriate, then I'd be happy to escort her myself."

A small drop of perspiration appeared at the director's temple. He wiped it away with his forefinger, leaving behind a small smudge of charcoal. Dr. Kingsley stiffened. He then walked slowly around Keble, as he spoke in a way that indicated he was pondering the proposal. "That might be a good idea..." Angelica noticed he was carefully eyeing the director's clipboard. Keble responded by turning the board away from the doctor, which gave her a perfect view of its contents. Several thick pages of charcoal drawings were sticking out slightly from behind the other papers. Keble stepped back abruptly and directed a hostile stare in Kingsley's direction.

"So..." the doctor whispered.

Angelica looked over Dr. Kingsley's shoulder, motioning to the two figures that had just entered the room behind him.

The doctor turned to see who had caught the young girl's attention.

He adopted a friendly tone, easing the growing tension.

Pam and the elderly priest approached the group. She gave Dr. Kingsley a warm smile, but her smile faded when she saw who was in his company.

She looked as though she were ready to say something unpleasant to the director but thankfully, at that moment, Aunt Dot, Liam, Serena, and Joachim also joined the group.

"Hello, Dr. Kingsley," Aunt Dot said warmly. "Dolly was adamant that I tell you how upset she was that she wasn't able to see you today."

"Yes," the doctor said sadly. "I was going to ask about her but got a little distracted." He scanned the group. "Is everyone else here?"

Aunt Dot shook her head. "Frankie's with Dolly back at the house, and Christian also decided to stay back and help with an...unexpected, emergency clean-up situation." The doctor raised his eyebrow and Dot added, "It's probably best you don't ask."

Joachim then spoke. "Christian's also going to read through some family history books," he said, happy to have something to contribute to the grown-up conversation. "He told me so."

Dr. Kingsley seemed lost in thought. "You know," he said abruptly, "I do feel quite bad that Dolly wasn't able to come. I hate to think of her disappointment." He looked at his watch. "I am due for lunch break soon, and the castle is really only about five minutes away....Yes," he said decidedly, turning to look at Aunt Dot, "if you don't think she'd mind, perhaps I'll drop in on her."

"Oh, you know she would love that!" Aunt Dot affirmed.

"Pam, if I may speak to you for a moment," the doctor said, leading the woman away from the group. He turned back to ensure there was enough distance from the others to assure their privacy.

"What is it, Dr. Kingsley?" Pam asked, her voice full of concern.

"Your sister had been drawing in her sketchbook. I had encouraged her to draw whenever she was sorting through difficult emotions, but also following her nightmares. I thought that, perhaps, if there was any foul play or anything odd, she would able to communicate it through the images, before she could no longer remember the incidents."

"That sounds like very helpful advice."

"I believed it was, but then I discovered that some of the

pages were missing, as though someone was trying to hide something."

"Someone stole her artwork?"

"Yes, and I just noticed the edges of some pages that look very much like your sister's work, attached to Roger Keble's clipboard."

"We should confront him."

"Actually, I have a plan. There is something I need to attend to, but upon my return, I will find a way to confiscate his clipboard and you will be my witness. Once we have the evidence, we can call the police. Proof that he has been stealing from the residents should be more than enough to have him removed. And then perhaps the patients will be safe from anything else he has been doing to harm them."

"I think we should approach him now," she stated.

"I don't think it's a good idea to do it with all the children around. The exchange could be quite upsetting. And I can't predict how he'll respond. I wouldn't want to put anyone at risk, should he panic."

"I understand," she sighed. "But soon, please, before he has a chance to dispose of the evidence."

He nodded and, as he went to leave, she gently grabbed his arm. "Dr. Kingsley, thank you. You said I could trust you to find a way to end whatever has been preventing Sophia's recovery, and you really came through."

He smiled reassuringly, and then hurriedly pulled out his keys and headed off to the exit.

Almost as soon as he left, Will, Allora, and Mary rushed into the common room.

"Grandma," Will called out to Pam. "We need you to see something right away."

"What is it?" she asked.

Mary turned to the director. "Hello again, Mr. Keble. Is there a more private room, maybe somewhere with a table, where we could all talk?"

"Yes, we have a meeting room that should be large enough to accommodate your group."

"Oh good," she said. "You should come too."

"I don't think that's a good idea," Pam insisted. St. John Henry approached her and spoke gently. "I think, perhaps, we should let the children lead us on this one."

"You don't understand," she said, her voice shaking with growing anxiety.

"Peace," the saint whispered, and she somehow allowed herself to be brought into the room without further objection.

As soon as everyone had gathered in, Mary closed the door and Will blurted out the story about the missing pages and the secret hiding place. The mention of the stolen pages had Pam fighting every urge to unleash her fury on Roger Keble.

"We had encouraged Aunt Sophia to draw in the book whenever she could, and to keep it hidden. Well, she did use the book, and look!" Will placed the book on the meeting room table and the company gathered around.

The first image showed the same dancers that the children remembered from the earlier drawings, but they had shrunk in size, and somehow now looked more like children. The shadowy creatures from the previous pages had all come together, forming one man... or at least the silhouette of a man who wore a crown atop his head. A hand was drawn at the side of his mouth, as though he were whispering into the ears of the small dancers. They were cowering, clearly terrified of the being.

The next page was very revealing. The shadow had turned and his features were now perfectly pronounced.

"No..." Pam whispered.

"There's no denying whose face that is," Allora stated. "It's Dr. Kingsley."

"And that's the evil throne in the woods," Joachim exclaimed, pointing to the background, where the twisted roots were clearly visible within a forested landscape.

"Wait," Liam said. "If that's the twisted throne from the diary, and there are images of the man wearing a crown, just as a 'kingship' had been mentioned in several entries, then that means the author of the diary and Kingsley..."

"Are one and the same," Serena whispered, her eyes wide and fearful.

"I can confirm the perpetrator is Dr. Kingsley," Roger Keble spoke, his voice shaking. "I found these just today in his office: the other pages. I suspected that something wasn't right with him. Often, after a visit from the doctor, we had discovered that patients were becoming more withdrawn and losing their ability to communicate. It has been something I had been wrestling with since we began to note a pattern. I'm afraid I wasn't very approachable during that time, and..." He looked in Pam's direction. "I apologize for not being ready or willing to discuss anything with concerned family members. I was ashamed that so many residents were being negatively impacted and I had no answers." He laid the pages on the table. "Kingsley may know that I have these. Perhaps I was a fool to keep them with me, but I didn't want to risk giving him the opportunity to destroy them."

He spread them out and everyone examined the images. Again the children saw the same man, clearly the doctor, but fitted with a crown. One drawing showed him standing over a black pond or river, where children were chained, imprisoned on fragmented rafts. Another detailed the man seated on his throne with black creatures asleep at his feet.

"I'm the fool," Pam muttered.

"He's fooled many people, especially Aunt Dolly," Serena said, sadly shaking her head.

"Wait!" Pam suddenly called out. "He's on his way to see Dolly right now. Can we warn her?"

"Dolly won't have her phone on her, and she'll be outside, still dealing with the mess from the chickens... again, don't ask. But perhaps we can try to call the house, and maybe we can catch Frankie or Christian."

CHAPTER 20

Christian had helped Aunt Dolly as much as he could, until she insisted he go inside and clean himself up. He washed his hands and changed his clothes before heading up to the library. He seated himself on the floor by the books and pulled out one entitled, *Mitchell Family History 1850-1950.* The book was quite large. It was hand-written and contained drawings of a coat of arms and an account of the history of the Mitchell family name.

Christian leafed through, past stories of an account of the land over which Lord William J. Mitchell's father had been lord, complete with drawings of his beautiful estate. The story of Lord William's voyage to America was included in the book, as were the specifications of the castle he had built for his pregnant wife.

Christian turned a few more pages, until he came across

a family tree. He ran his finger over the drawing as he read the names of Lord William J. Mitchell's descendants.

Lord William J. Mitchell 1854 - 1940	married	Eleanor M. (née Richards) 1860-1933
Rachel D. Mitchell 1882-1937	married	John C. Kingsley 1879-1933
David M. Kingsley 1911-	married	Christine E. (née Taylor) 1917-
George C. Kingsley 1948-		

He froze, a million thoughts rushing through his mind. *George Kingsley is Lord William J. Mitchell's great grandson. That means the man who lost the castle in a single hand of cards...was his father. Why wouldn't he have told us who he was, or the truth about his history with the castle?*

Just then he heard some voices coming from the hallway. One he recognized right away as Kingsley himself. He quickly pushed the book back onto the shelf. He wasn't sure how the doctor would react to his having found out the truth and he wasn't willing to find out. He panicked and quickly grabbed another book randomly, then sat on one of the bottom steps of the spiral staircase and started to read.

Aunt Frankie led Dr. Kingsley into the library. Christian closed his book and stood up to greet the doctor. "Oh, hi, Dr. Kingsley," he said, hoping the overly chipper tone of his voice wouldn't reveal his nervousness.

The doctor smiled warmly, glancing over at the section holding the family archives.

"I was just reading," the boy offered.

Dr. Kingsley scanned the book in Christian's hand. "And you enjoy reading about *Unusual Fungal Infections of the Toe*?"

"Yes," he replied, his voice sounding a little screechy. "It's a very recently acquired interest. Apparently, you can treat toe fungus with cinnamon."

"Really?"

"Yup. As long as it's organic."

"Ah," the doctor said with a quick nod. "I just came from the seniors' home and saw your siblings. Your younger brother said you were going to be reading some books about Lord Mitchell's family history."

"I do find genealogy pretty fascinating," Christian answered, "but I think I should finish reading about toe funguses first. Maybe I'll get into more of the family archives afterwards."

The teenager smiled, as though satisfied with his cover story, and added, "Maybe I should go check on Aunt Dolly now." He paused. "She might need more help cleaning up the chicken coop."

"I'll come with you. I'd be happy to help," Dr. Kingsley said.

"It's very kind of you to offer, but you might want to sit this one out," Aunt Frankie asserted. "It's a big mess and it's going to be a lot of work to clean it up."

"I'm not afraid of hard work," the doctor assured her. "I'm not a scobberlotcher," he added chuckling.

"I have no idea what that means," Aunt Frankie admitted.

"It's an old English term for a lazy person who seems allergic to work."

"And here I thought it might have been a made-up word you picked up from Dot," she said with a smile, raising an eyebrow.

The two were heading out of the library, but they paused to look back at Christian, who was again frozen in thought.

"Are you coming?" Aunt Frankie asked the boy.

"Yes," he mustered. "Sorry, yes, I'm coming."

He followed his aunt and Dr. Kingsley, but his mind was in overdrive. Where had he heard that word before: *scobberlotcher*. It was so familiar. He racked his brain.

How do I know that word? Think, Christian, think. Wait. The diary. It was used in the diary. What are the odds?

He continued his thought process. *So, Dr. Kingsley is the son of the man who lost the castle. They must have been financially devastated. Kingsley probably didn't know it was lost in a poker game, and that would explain why he was so shocked and angry when Aunt Dolly mentioned it. If the house was lost in 1955, and Kingsley was born in 1948, then he probably lived here until he was seven years old. He knew that there had once been a hatch in the tower. What else does he know? His father would have known about the bunkhouse in the woods, and it's possible that they could have moved there for the winter of 1962–1963. Scobberlotcher. Dr. Kingsley must have hated his father, blaming him for their financial ruin. It fits. Dr. Kingsley must be the boy in the woods...the boy in the diary who threatened to return and take over everything.*

He slowed his pace, somehow needing just a little more distance between Kingsley and himself. Aunt Frankie periodically turned around to check on him as they continued through the kitchen and out the porch door. They could see the coop from the veranda. It was about fifty feet away and Aunt Dolly's happy screech could be heard loud and clear: "GEORGIE!!!" She waved her arms frantically. "YOU MIGHT WANT TO STAY BACK, MY LOVE!"

Dr. Kingsley descended the stairs and made his way to Dolly. He held his nose tightly, but nobly took the hose from Dolly's hand. Aunt Frankie hung back with Christian. "Are you going to tell me what's going on?"

The boy nodded and began to open his mouth, but just then the phone began to ring.

"I'm going to go get that," his aunt said, walking back to the kitchen. "But then we're going to have a little talk."

CHAPTER 21

The van raced down the dirt driveway. Liam had to slow the vehicle, as it was getting difficult to see anything with the dust rising all around. He was clearly frustrated.

"It's alright, Liam," Serena assured her brother. "Aunt Frankie said she'll keep an eye on Dr. Kingsley until we all get there."

Allora frowned, deep in thought. "I feel like we should have a plan in place," she said.

Serena leaned over and said, "We have something better: a saint."

Serena looked over at the extra passenger in their van. She felt sure that having "Fr. John Henry" with them meant that everything would somehow be alright. The saint caught her eye and winked, his smile warm and reassuring.

Will's car was right behind theirs. He had Aunt Dot with

him. His grandmother had decided to stay back with the director. They would be searching Kingsley's office and the patient files of all those who were being kept in the east wing, as well as those, like Sophia, who were showing signs of despondency. They were hoping to find enough evidence to prove the doctor's wrongdoings.

When the group arrived at the castle, they were met by Christian, who readily opened the gate.

"Aunt Frankie is serving Dr. Kingsley tea in the great room. Aunt Dolly will be meeting us there after she has a shower. She didn't smell too good after tending the chickens."

Aunt Dot's face was tight with impending rage. "I hate to think of that villain sitting in my great room, trying to manipulate my baby sister!"

Christian took a deep breath. "Actually, he probably feels like it's HIS great room—or that it should be anyway." Aunt Dot gave him a puzzled look as he continued: "I was able to check the family archives and it turns out that Kingsley is actually Lord WIlliam J. Mitchell's great grandson! It was his father who lost the castle to your grandfather. I've been wondering if his 'relationship' with Aunt Dolly is part of his plan to regain what he believes should rightfully be his."

Aunt Dot was stunned, and then her face filled with sadness. "Oh, that must have been very hard for him: losing his home. I'm ashamed that I never thought of it before: that our grandfather's good fortune came at such a terrible cost for the man who lost to him. I never stopped to think that he might have had a family."

But the moment of sympathy ended abruptly when she remembered the images she had seen at the seniors' home.

"He lied to us all! And he's hurt so many people. It was wrong for his father to have gambled away the castle, but the harm he has caused so many people is also VERY, VERY wrong. He has to go!"

Mary sighed. "But we can't just barge in there with all our accusations. We don't know how he'll react. He's kind of a loose cannon." She turned to the saint and asked, "What should we do?"

Aunt Dot very subtly leaned over, whispering to Liam, "Why are we asking the priest we just met at the seniors' home again? And why did we bring him home with us?"

He whispered back, "You saw how evil the drawings were. Don't you think it's a good idea to have a priest around?"

She thought for a moment and then readily agreed.

"Come," the saint said, taking Aunt Dot's arm and leading the group across the bridge and toward the castle.

Meanwhile, Aunt Frankie was doing her best to keep the doctor entertained.

While Dr. Kingsley and Dolly had been finishing up with the chickens, she had managed to go through the Mitchell family history book in the library. She had found the family tree and had carefully torn it from the book. She knew that she would need to keep it safe from the doctor, lest he attempt to destroy the evidence. Frankie was also convinced that Dolly would need to see the family tree with her own eyes, or else there would be no way she'd believe her sisters, especially if it would mean losing the *love of her life*.

The doctor sat on the loveseat, casually leaning back and sipping his tea. A plate of cookie crumbs sat on his lap, as he had polished off two of the love-offerings from Dolly. The woman herself was absent, declaring she needed to make herself presentable after all her time with the chickens. Aunt Frankie knew that Dolly would be taking a very long time, as prettying herself up for her beau was a complicated and laborious task.

She glanced over at the small side table by the sofa. Kingsley's love token from the day before, the bouquet of flowers, was prominently displayed within Aunt Dot's abhorrent banana vase. Frankie's young niece had told her about Kingsley's aversion to the work of horror. She was hoping his repulsion would mean he would be staying far away from it, especially since that is exactly where she had hidden the rolled-up page from the coveted book. She did notice he refused to make eye contact with the object.

He broke the silence with a casual sigh. "You know," he said lightly, "I've been thinking about your library upstairs, and I was wondering if it would be possible for me spend a little more time going through some of its books. I would imagine your sister might still be a while yet. If it would be alright with you, I'd like to perhaps borrow a book or two. I promise I will take good care of them and will return the items promptly."

"Sure," Aunt Frankie said, rising to her feet. "We can go there now."

He raised a hand in her direction. "Oh no, please don't feel obliged to accompany me. I'm sure I can find my way, and I wouldn't want to trespass on your time."

"It's really not an imposition," Aunt Frankie dryly assured him.

"No, but really," he insisted. "I had told your sister that I would be here when she was finished getting ready, and I would hate for her to arrive only to find an empty room."

A shrilly, girlish voice filled the room.

"Oh, Georgie!" Aunt Dolly exclaimed. "You are so thoughtful! How sweet of you to worry about your little girlfriend. It's alright though; I'm here, my love!"

Dr. Kingsley forced a smile. "Wonderful," he said.

Aunt Dolly hurried to Kingsley's side. She glanced around the room, beaming, until her eyes fell on the bouquet of flowers. Her smile faded and she sighed sympathetically. "Oh no, my beautiful flowers. They look so thirsty. Let me just go get them some water."

"No," Frankie shot out abruptly.

Dr. Kingsley eyed her carefully. She quickly recovered. "As you may have overheard, Dr. Kingsley was just saying he'd like to go to the library, and perhaps borrow a few books. Now that you're here, I thought you might like to take him. I can water your flowers for you."

"Aw, thank you, Frankie," Aunt Dolly said, as she hooked her arm through her boyfriend's and led him out of the great room.

Dr. Kingsley turned back, eyeing the woman who stood tall and perfectly still, her arms crossed over her chest. Her look was that of one poised for an impending battle.

CHAPTER 22

Dolly merrily made her way into the library, trying to hide how tired she was from the climb up the stairs. "You probably already know which books you'd like to borrow, buuuuut, there are also some amazing books over here that you may not have seen." She reached up to a shelf across the room from the family archives.

"Oh yes," she said cheerfully. "Here it is!" She pulled out a large, colorful book and handed it to Kingsley. He looked down and cleared his throat, before reading the title aloud. "*How to Guarantee that She'll Say YES: 50 of the Best Marriage Proposal Ideas to Get Your Girl*" His eyebrows could not have lifted any higher as he turned his attention to Aunt Dolly. "This is very nice," he whispered, still unable to lower his eyebrows. "Thank you. I would definitely like to borrow this... this special book." Dolly squeezed his arm, her smile so wide it seemed to reach her earlobes.

The doctor glanced over at the family archives. "My darling," he said. "I hate to ask this, but I am as parched as your bouquet of flowers downstairs. Would you be so kind as to get me a drink? It can be anything really."

"Iced tea?"

"I would absolutely love iced tea."

Aunt Dolly sighed. "And I will absolutely get you that drink, but if I'm panting a little...or a lot, when I come back up, just know that it's not because I'm out of shape or anything; it's because being near you makes my heart flutter so much... and my breath gets really heavy, and sweat starts forming pretty much everywhere...but it's more like liquid love drops...and, it's just because of the effect you have on me. Again, nothing to do with being out of shape."

"Of course," the doctor replied. "I feel the same way about you."

She smiled and was on her way.

As soon as she left the room, Kingsley rushed over to the family archives. He pulled out the book he knew would contain information about his family's history, and searched for the image of Lord Mitchell's family tree. The pages had been numbered, and as he flipped through them to the section he knew would contain the coveted drawing, he was at a loss to discover that it was missing. He slammed the book shut and shoved it back onto the shelf. Where was it? His eyes scanned shelf and the area just beneath the book, leading to his discovery of a few tiny fragments of paper sitting on the floor. They bore the same aged characteristics as Lord Mitchell's family history book. He picked up a piece and examined it. Clearly someone had torn the page out very recently. The boy? No; the doctor was convinced he wouldn't have ripped a page out of the book without consulting his aunt. *His aunt*. Frankie. She was definitely acting more guarded when he had returned from the chicken coop with Dolly.

His train of thought was interrupted by a myriad of visitors. *Wonderful*, he thought, clenching his teeth. The children all entered the room, along with Aunt Dot, Frankie, and the old priest he had seen at the seniors' home.

Aunt Dot stepped forward, the saint still at her side. "Have you been introduced to Father John Henry?" she asked him.

"No," the doctor said, in a light, courteous tone. "I don't believe I've had the pleasure."

The saint nodded. "No, and I would not deprive you of it," he said teasingly. Under his breath, he continued, "Being that its pursuit has been your life's sole focus."

"I'm sorry?" the doctor said. "I couldn't make out..."

St. John Henry raised a hand and said, "It was nothing, just the mumblings of a silly old man." The saint inspected the library. "This is quite the collection of valuable information, is it not?"

"Yes," the man said, nodding while fighting off a sudden urge to take flight.

Dolly entered the room, huffing and puffing away. She held a glass of iced tea in one hand, while the other clamped a plate of cookies.

She handed the glass to the doctor and turned excitedly to the priest. "Hello! Are you from a nearby parish?" The saint began to answer but was quickly cut off by the excited aunt. "Because if you are, there's a chance we may be needing your services in the near future," she said, winking at Kingsley. "My parish priest might still be mad at me for a little misunderstanding involving holy water, so I'd like to keep my options open." She suddenly had a thought. "Georgie, you are Catholic, right?"

The doctor nodded his head. "Yes, though a little out of practice."

St. John Henry raised an eyebrow. "So, perhaps Catholic in name only."

Kingsley looked appalled. "I assure you, I am well versed in Scripture."

Newman nodded before bluntly replying, "As is the devil."

Dolly let out a strange squeak, and in an attempt to break the growing tension, extended the plate of cookies to Kingsley.

"Have another, my love."

The doctor patted his stomach lightly. "Oh, I couldn't in good conscience."

Newman winced. "It would be best not to use that phrase so lightly. A good conscience, I would submit, is ordered to the truth. Perhaps you should instead say, 'I could, as I am governed by my own self will, but as it stands, I am inclined to decline.' Yes, I think that would be much more appropriate in that it would be...accurate."

Kingsley frowned slightly, thrown off by the visitor's forthright comments.

Aunt Dolly walked across the room where there was a small desk and chair. She set the plate on the desk and motioned for the children and the others to come and help themselves to the cookies. Aunt Frankie stood resolutely at the entrance to the library. Aunt Dolly approached her, chastising her older sister. "You told me you were going to water my flowers, but when I stopped by the great room for a little flower-sniffing pick-me-upper, I could tell you hadn't."

Aunt Frankie looked very concerned. She hushed her sister and whispered. "You didn't water them, did you?"

Aunt Dolly was not picking up on her sister's cues encouraging her to lower her voice, and so she continued, "I went to water them, but there was a paper in the vase. I put the bouquet in a new vase instead, but why on earth is there an old..." Frankie placed her hand over Dolly's mouth.

Just then there was a loud click, as though something—a door or window—had swung shut. Frankie scanned the room before wondering out loud, "Where is Dr. Kingsley?"

St. John Henry Newman walked over to the bookshelf where Kingsley had been standing just before. "It would seem the roach has taken to the walls," he said matter-of-factly.

"Another secret passageway?" Angelica asked, as she felt along the books.

"Indeed."

Liam approached the bookshelf. "Do you remember the first day Dr. Kingsley came to visit? I noticed that he had lightly fiddled with these books up here, on the middle shelf." Liam began to pull each book, one by one, until he came across a thick novel whose bottom remained fixed to the shelf. He tilted it back sharply and heard a slight click, as an entire section of the bookshelf swung open: a secret door opening to a passage behind.

Angelica sighed. "I wish we weren't all so distracted by the cookies. We could have stopped him from escaping." She hesitantly took a step into space beyond the door, looking for the escapee. "So cool!" she cried out, sticking her head back into library and exclaiming excitedly, "It's a slide!"

Joachim ran to the opening, "I want to try it!" He hesitated. "But where does it go?"

Aunt Frankie joined them at the bookshelf. "I think he may have overheard Dolly talking about the page I ripped out detailing his relation to Lord Mitchell. Maybe he's going to look for it."

"WHAT?!" Aunt Dolly looked absolutely flabbergasted. "What is going on? You think my Georgie is a relative of Lord Mitchell?"

Aunt Frankie spoke frankly. "He's his great grandson. He

lived here years ago and seems to be trying to work his way back into the castle. Why else do you think he's been pouring the flattery and attention on so thickly?"

"Because HE LOVES ME!" Aunt Dolly huffed. "And I'm not sure I believe you. He would have told me if he had a connection to the castle. We're soul mates."

"No, you're not," Aunt Frankie said, rolling her eyes.

"That's it!" Aunt Dolly cried out, dashing over to the bookshelf and squeezing her way through the opening. "I'm coming, my love!" The group could hear the echo of her voice as she threw herself down the slide. "Ohhhhh myyyyyy!"

Suddenly, she was perfectly silent, and then they heard her call out, "Um...hello? So, it seems that I might be an itsy, bitsy, bitty-bit stuck."

"You've got to be kidding me," Aunt Frankie said, fully exasperated.

"I would LOVE to be kidding you, but no, not so much. Definitely stuck."

Frankie leaned into the opening beyond the bookshelf. "Do you want us to send some of the children down the slide?"

"I'm near the end...I think," Aunt Dolly called up. "I think it would be better if someone pulled me out from the bottom."

"That would be fine, if we knew where the bottom was!"

Christian interrupted. "I think I might know where the slide ends. When we were giving Dr. Kingsley a tour of the castle, I noticed him knocking on the wall beside Lord William J. Mitchell's painting in the stairwell. I can run downstairs and check and see if that's where it ends."

Aunt Frankie agreed. "I'll stay here. The rest of you go too, and maybe some of you could quickly head over to the great room. Thanks to Dolly, I'm convinced Dr. Kingsley knows exactly where I hid the family tree."

CHAPTER 23

Christian stood before the panel in the stairwell. He knocked on the wall and could hear the muted rustling of someone just beyond.

"I think this is it, but I don't know how to open it. Dr. Kingsley probably used a latch from inside, but I have no idea how to open it from this side of the wall."

Mary reached up and touched Lord Mitchell's portrait. "The last hidden door handle was behind the painting of the Mystical Rose," she said. "Maybe this painting is also the key."

Will helped her lift the painting off the wall. Behind it, there was another wooden accent. It bore the image of the Mitchell family crest: three upside-down shells separated by a large inverted *V*.

St. John Henry approached the image. He turned to Will. "Does this remind you of anything?"

"Yes," Will said, pulling out his chain bearing Newman's crest. He thought for a moment. "You know, if I were to turn all the shells upwards, they would look a lot like the hearts that are on your crest."

"Yes, I agree," the saint said, his eyes twinkling.

Will reached up and, sure enough, he was able to rotate the three shells. Once the last shell had been altered, the large panel in front of Christian slid open and the shells shot back to their original position.

Inside, they could see Aunt Dolly's legs flailing. Her fuzzy slippers were thrashing around in a frenzied panic.

Angelica and Christian reached out and grabbed the bottom half of her legs, pulling with all their might. Inch by inch, they budged her; finally they were able to pull her down the remainder of the slide toward the opening. "She's almost out!" Christian cried.

Aunt Dot placed her hand on Mary's shoulder. "Now that I know they can get her out, I think some of us should follow your Aunt Frankie's advice of heading over to the great room. I hate to think of that awful man in the same room as my beautiful banana vase." Mary agreed to join her, as did Will, Liam, Allora, Joachim, and St. John Henry.

They flew to the room as quickly as they could and, upon entering, Aunt Dot gasped in horror. "PUT DOWN MY VASE!" she cried out.

The doctor held the vase out, just in front of him. He sighed. "I guess it's no use now, anyway. You won't need its content to convince your sister of who I am. But I'm afraid I'll need you to allow me to leave undeterred. And to assure my safe departure, I will keep this...abomination, as my hostage. One move and I won't hesitate to smash it to bits."

Aunt Dot's mouth dropped open. "Are you even human!?"

The saint stepped forward. "I assure you he is human, but he is actuated by very different spirits than the One who governs our hearts and actions."

Kingsley heaved an annoyed sigh. "I don't know who you are, but I have no time for an utter dotard's incessant driveling." He walked over to the bookcase opposite the wall of the fireplace. He began pulling on the books midway up the shelf. "Now, where is it?" he muttered to himself.

"What are you doing?" Aunt Dot questioned the man.

"I know there's a passageway here. I remember Grandma telling me that her father had one built in this very room. She told me it would lead to hidden treasure chests." He shot a look at Aunt Dot. "Your grandfather stripped my family of everything. I think it only fair that I am given something in return."

Aunt Dot took a step toward him. He held the vase up in the air, his eyes fierce and threatening. "Everyone get back, or I promise you this vase will be shattered beyond repair."

Aunt Dot pouted. "I hope you know that if you destroy my vase, a piece of my soul will be crushed with it."

St. John Henry placed his hand gently on her shoulder. "Once this hostile situation deescalates, I believe we should have a little discussion about inappropriate attachments."

Aunt Dot shrugged sheepishly.

"My dear sir," he continued, turning his attention to Dr. Kingsley, "I can assure you that the contents of the trunks you seek will not enrich your life in the manner you would assume. They are gifts freely given, but you are not in a state that would allow you access to their benefits."

"Honestly," Kingsley cried out in frustration. "Is there no escape from your incessant commentary?"

"I apologize," the saint replied. "I am ever compelled to speak the Truth."

The doctor seemed to growl under his breath, but he ignored the saint and continued wiggling and pulling on books. In his frustration, he grabbed the entire bookcase with his free hand and began to shake it violently. A couple of books fell from the very top shelf, just missing Kingsley's head. The frantic doctor barely seemed to take notice as he shook the unit harder and harder. Liam noticed the infamous butterfly-frog-rock creation moving slowly to the edge of the top shelf. His eyes widened as he issued Kingsley a warning. "You might want to take it easy on that thing."

Dr. Kingsley ignored the boy and shook the bookshelf harder still. The group of witnesses winced deeply as the large rock plummeted down in a shower of glitter, smacking the oblivious man squarely on the head. He seemed frozen in confusion for a split second, then fell to the floor.

THUD! SMASH! "NOOOOOOOOOOOOO!"

Poor Aunt Dot ran to her vanquished vase, mourning the broken banana. She then found her humanity and turned to Dr. Kingsley. He had been completely knocked out.

Liam and the saint carefully lifted the doctor onto the sofa.

"OH, WOW!" The voice was Christian's as he entered the room with Aunt Dolly and the others. "What happened here?"

"Oh, my poor Georgie!" Aunt Dolly cried out as she ran to Kingsley's side.

Joachim frowned. "You know that he's a total bad guy, right?"

"Here's the proof," Aunt Dot said, sniffling as she pulled out the family tree from the remnants of the shattered vase. "A great sacrifice was made to bring you the truth."

Aunt Dolly sighed, "I know. Angelica has been filling me in about how he hasn't been forthcoming, and that apparently he's been manipulating, plotting, ruining lives, et cetera, but I can't help feeling bad for him."

She plopped herself down on the floor beside the sofa and gently inspected his head. "Oh, that's a lot of glitter," she mused. She turned to the saint. "Will he be alright?"

He nodded. "He will recover. However, he will remain unconscious for quite some time. In fact, he will almost choose to be so, as it is when he is asleep that he enters his dark kingdom." He turned his attention to the children. "The time has come to embark on our mission. Dr. Kingsley has retreated into the world of his creation. We will meet him there. As he feels he has lost his bid in securing a physical dominion over these parts, he will be ever more diligent in assuring he retains his kingship over the prisoners bound to his imagination. We will take to the secret passageway. There are items in the sealed trunks that will be of great assistance for the task at hand."

Aunt Dot cleared her throat, and the saint couldn't help smiling at the two aunts who stared at the group, looking as though the old man had just informed them that they would be sprouting wings and fighting monkey-faced squids.

He smiled compassionately. "I apologize. I would imagine that this all must seem so shocking and fantastical to you, but I cannot faithfully express the importance of this quest, in which you also must play a part."

Oddly enough, Aunt Dolly looked intrigued and enamored by the prospect, although she stated bluntly, "I would rather not go through any more passageways for a while. I've had my fill."

"No," he assured her. "I will tell you exactly what will be required of you."

He walked over to the bookshelf and bent low, pulling the antique book that unlocked the door. Liam beckoned the others to join him at the painting of the Mystical Rose, as he lifted it and set it to the side.

Newman encouraged the children to head to the hidden cave containing the trunks. He assured them that he would soon join them after he had finished giving the aunts their instructions.

Just then, Aunt Frankie entered the room, gripping her wooden spoon. "Don't worry. I'll keep an eye on Dr. Kingsley," she assured the children as they made their way into the secret passageway. Angelica was the last to enter. She turned back and waved to the aunts. She couldn't help smiling as she saw Aunt Frankie standing over Kingsley, smacking the wooden spoon against her hand.

CHAPTER 24

They hurried along the path, down the stairs, and through the secret stone doorway. As they rushed, Allora couldn't help thinking about the tiny tunnel that would be their exit from the cave. Just the thought of the confined space made her throat tighten and her stomach feel a little queasy.

Once in the cave, Liam went straight to the two locked trunks. He knelt before one while Christian approached the other. They pushed the buttons in the proper sequence:

JESUS, CHRIST, GOD'S SON, SAVIOR

In a beautiful explosion of vibrant light, the trunks flung open.

"I have been simmering with anticipation for this moment!" St. John Henry joyfully exclaimed as he entered the cavern. "Quickly, reach in and take your garments from the first trunk. You will be clothing yourself in a similar fashion to those you are being sent to free. Kingsley has dressed them as his peasants, and in his emphatic insanity, has stolen years of wisdom from his subjects to ensure they are most vulnerable to him. He will not permit an uprising or chance that they would fully remember who they once were. They will all look as children, and so among them, enshrined in your own youthfulness, you will be less likely to draw attention to yourselves."

"Wait," Will interrupted. "So my Aunt Sophia will look like a little girl?"

"Yes," the saint admitted. "She will likely not recognize you, and she will not be able to speak, as he has rendered all of his prisoners voiceless, but she will readily accept your help."

"How will we communicate with them if they can't speak?" Allora asked.

"Will has been given a most necessary gift. He will be able to speak to their hearts and, within his own heart, their voices will resound."

"Can you tell us about the gifts of the Holy Spirit that each of us has been given?" Allora inquired.

"With great pleasure." The saint turned his attention to Liam. "The gift you will have access to for this mission is WISDOM. You have been given the monocle because this particular gift will offer you a heavenly perspective. You will be able to recognize the truth. If you find yourself suspecting that something is amiss, or perhaps an illusion, through the glass the truth will be revealed." Liam nodded, examining the precious item.

"Allora, your gift is UNDERSTANDING. The locket around your neck, once opened, will unleash a brilliant light. Not only will it light the way, but it can also penetrate through obstinate objects."

"Like a laser," Allora mused.

The saint smiled. "It is very powerful. Understanding helps illuminate the mind to truth. It offers profound insight and deep penetration into divine truths of the faith. I am confident you will use this gift well."

He turned to Joachim. "Joachim, you have been given COUNSEL. Almost by intuition, you will have a sense of what course of action you should be taking. The compass you were given represents that connection you have to the Holy Spirit, in that He will always be there, guiding you. If you feel you have lost your way, look to this wholly reliable, infallible gift, as counsel will always point you in the right direction."

The boy grinned in response. "I can lead everybody," he declared proudly.

"Angelica, you must be perfectly confused by your gift," St. John Henry said to the girl.

"Yeah," she admitted. "It's kind of weird that it's just a stone...although it's magnetized, so that's cool."

"Your gift is FORTITUDE. It is courage, strength, and fearlessness, all which you possess in great measure. Do not let the size of your gift fool you, for a giant was slain by a small boy with just such an item. Your stone, however, will not remain as it is now. As with the nature of courage, it grows and strengthens. Your small rock can make formations. It can become a shield, body armor, or whatever your imagination allows you to create, so that you may rise up to face the evil at hand."

Her mouth dropped open. "Amazing! Okay, I love my gift now."

"Mary," the saint said, gesturing to the gloves she had placed on her hands. "You have received the gift of KNOWLEDGE. This incredible gift helps people recognize in every created thing the God who fashioned them. Our foe, in his bizarre world, has twisted God's creations, turning them into obstacles: barriers preventing God's children from the union they so desire with him. You will use these gloves to reorder those creations back to that which God intended them to be. Your touch will remind the creation of its true Creator. I cannot express enough the importance of your gift in the knave's lair of illusion."

Mary beamed, "I can't wait to try it!"

"Serena, it is no surprise that the Holy Spirit chose to grace you with the gift of PIETY. Yours is a tender devotion to Our Lord, stemming from a deep, constant, and faithful love for all he has given us, especially through the Church. Just as every ailment has its specific treatment or cure, every evil you will face has a prayer or action that would prove most effective in quickly squelching its attack and quashing the effects of its poison.

Your devotion, symbolized by the heart-shaped ruby around your neck, will allow you to access the perfect prayer, verse, or action, by simply holding the object and bowing your head in prayer. Our Church holds a trove of treasures, a full arsenal to combat evil."

Serena smiled shyly, overwhelmed by the gift she had been given.

"Lastly, Christian, who holds the gift of THE FEAR OF THE LORD."

Christian stepped forward, displaying his golden rope, looped at his waist. "Why a rope?" he blurted out. "What can this thing do?"

The saint laughed, still fully amused by the boy's forthcoming nature.

"The fear of the Lord allows us a perfect connection to Our Lord. Someone who fears the Lord wants nothing more than to live according to God's holy will. The rope is a perfect representation of this connection—this desire to be tethered to the Almighty. You will discover how this gift will be made manifest through your creativity within Kingsley's false world."

"Okay," Christian said, nodding. "I'm still a little unclear, but I guess I'll just trust that I'll know how to use it when the time comes."

"And so you shall. The Holy Spirit will direct you."

He cleared his throat and then addressed the children.

"You each have a very important and unique role to play. You were created by God, with a very clear purpose in mind. He has made that perfectly evident by placing these trunks here, long before you were even born, waiting years and years for your arrival."

He gestured to the trunks. "After you have dressed in your garments, your footwear will seek you."

"Our footwear?" Mary asked. "Wait! Is it the same footwear that we were given in our last mission? The part of the armor of God that included our feet being fitted with the Gospel of Peace?"

The saint nodded.

"Ooooh," Mary squealed, jumping up and down with excitement. "So, we can run super-fast without getting tired....Oh, but we were dressed more like soldiers." She held her garment up against her chest. It was a long, glowing, but somewhat simple white gown. She frowned slightly. "I'm not sure the cool battle-ready boots will go with my outfit."

"I am sure the footwear will complement your attire to perfection. The Gospel of Peace is always in style, and it will bring you swiftly to your destination. You will be the bearers of the light and peace of Christ to each desolate soul."

Each of the children held their garments up against their chests. The saint instructed them to spin around three times in honor of the Most Holy Trinity. They did so, and upon the final turn they were miraculously dressed in the luminescent attire. From the second trunk, seemingly holographic footwear flew with great speed to each member, instantly clamping their feet in a flash of bluish light.

Mary gazed at her tall, slender, laced boots. She nodded in approval. The girls couldn't help swirling in their delicate, white gowns, and the boys wore short, white seamless tunics and light cotton pants. Each was given a belt and satchel. Christian swiftly attached his rope to the belt, and Liam was grateful to have something to carry his sandwich bag and lighter.

"Your garments have been blessed and they will prevent Kingsley from sensing your presence, until the time has come to face him directly. Now, we can no longer delay our entry into his world."

Allora winced, looking up at the hole near the ceiling. Angelica looked excited. "So, I guess we get to have a little swim first."

"No, my child," the saint replied. "We will not be going that way." Allora breathed a deep sigh of relief. "Through here," he said, as he walked over to a fixture on the wall that held a glowing torch. He removed the torch and turned the fixture clockwise. A loud crack followed by a gentle rumble filled the space as another rock doorway slid open.

Liam frowned. "You mean we could have exited the cave without squeezing through a tunnel and swimming into the river?"

Angelica shrugged. "Oops! I guess so, but then we would have missed out on all the fun."

The children followed St. John Henry through the opening. They were surprised to find that it led them to the chamber behind the falls. The two large metal panels still stood open, and the saint led them through the doors and along the tunnel to his quarters.

Once everyone was inside, Christian asked, "Is the door to Kingsley's world in here?"

"No, but follow me and we will soon be there," the saint replied, as he walked over to the fireplace. He pulled down on a small statue that sat upon the mantle. It must have been a lever, for almost at once the flames disappeared and the back of the fireplace opened up to a large hallway.

"I think I'm having déjà vu," Mary mused, as she looked down the hallway that seemed infinitely long. It was narrow and both sides were lined with a series of doors of varying styles and colors.

FLIFT, FLIFT, FLIFT, FLIFT...

The sound echoed down the hallway as torches were almost magically ignited one after the other.

Will shook his head in amazement. "This is incredible."

"Our door is a bit of a distance, but I am confident you will enjoy this auspicious opportunity to make use of your illustrious footwear," St. John Henry said with a smile.

"*Yes*!" Angelica cried out, as she dashed ahead. Immediately she was flooded with memories of the sensation of running with vivacious speed. One step in these boots seemed equal to ten, as the ground itself became a blurred conveyer belt under the light grazing of her feet. She shot forward, filled with wonder at the streak of lights and colors from the elements in her periphery.

The others joined her. Serena's hair trilled behind her, the speed and excitement causing her cheeks to glow. She felt as though she could run forever; however, within moments, St. John Henry's voice filled their thoughts and they were urged to stop.

With a little difficulty, the children managed to screech to a halt, sending a puff of dirt up into the air. Once the dust had settled, the children found themselves facing an old, wooden door. It looked like something from a medieval painting, looming and ominous. Joachim turned to the door on the opposite wall behind him. It was made of a frosted crystal, and looked almost heavenly.

"Can we go through this one instead?" he asked, pointing to the beautiful structure.

"I am sorry, my boy, but that door is presently locked to us. This one is the entry point to your imminent mission," he said.

Joachim sighed in disappointment. The saint patted his head before turning to the door and raising his hand. He prayed earnestly, his eyes closed tightly, his lips moving in a quickened whisper. As he finished, he blessed the door, his hand moving in the sign of the cross.

His eyes shot open and he breathed deeply as he approached a metal block with a latch, which was mounted on the door. There was a small keyhole and the saint promptly produced a large, iron key, which fit perfectly within. As he turned the key and lifted the latch, the door slowly opened.

CHAPTER 25

Almost as soon as the door opened, a foul-smelling fog rolled out to meet them. They stepped through the doorway into what appeared to be a swampy, densely entangled forest. It was lit by pale moonlight, and the children heard eerie sounds: a symphony of insects, howls, and far-off screeches of birds of prey.

The ground was slightly spongy, and any movement required the group to break apart sharp, thickly twisted branches. Serena reached out and a thorny vine pierced the side of her hand. Her hand shot back and she examined the cut. It was small, but she vowed to be more careful.

"Allora," the saint whispered. "We will be robbed of much time and energy if we continue to wrestle our way through all of these entanglements. If you wouldn't mind terribly, perhaps you could assist us by using your special gift."

Allora thought for a moment. "Maybe I could cut through all of these branches with my light."

He nodded, and everyone took a step back as Allora gently lifted the locket. She carefully faced the pendant toward the mass of thorny branches and opened the locket. Immediately a brilliant ray shot forth: a stream of burning light that easily sliced through the barriers that were preventing their advance. She held it steady, slowly pressing forward, creating a straight path. The others followed the girl as she pushed ahead. Finally, there was a clearing, and they found themselves working their way up a wide, grassy knoll.

They walked to the top and stood in horror, as they were faced with a giant, curved, grotesque wall, at least 100 feet tall. Thorny vines seemed alive, slithering and moving along the sides of the structure. A sickly, greenish fog poured over its rim. As they looked to the left and right, the children observed that the wall was incredibly long.

"It appears to be a circle," Liam said, adjusting his glasses. "And I would estimate its diameter to be at least a mile long."

"This is the border of Kingsley's kingdom. You are correct, it is an impenetrable circular monstrosity," the saint informed Liam. "There are no doors, for he controls who enters, and no one is permitted to leave."

"So, how do we get in?" Will asked.

"Can we use my light again?" Allora asked.

"I do not believe that would be an advisable course of action," the saint replied. "A breach of the walls would be most difficult, as they are fifteen feet thick, not to mention most noticeable. It would assuredly alert our foe to our presence. No, first we will need to find the safest point of entry: a place that will put us in a favorable position. Joachim will be our leader."

"Yes!" the boy cried out, lifting his fist and pumping it. He reached into his shirt, pulling at the chain, and produced the compass. "Follow me!" he said, as he held the object out in front of him.

The group gathered behind the small boy, who was busy examining his gift. "Holy Spirit, please show us where to go," the boy prayed. A swirl of light whisked its way around the circumference of the gold object. It spun faster and faster, until the fine needle at its center moved assuredly into a fixed position. Joachim began to move in the direction indicated by the needle. His pace quickened and the others followed suit, trekking along the top of the knoll. Finally, after what must have been about a half of a mile's travel (but with their footwear took a few short minutes), the compass rose just above Joachim's hand, spinning midair.

"What's it doing?" Joachim asked St. John Henry.

"It is indicating that we have arrived at our destination," the saint replied.

The children observed the area to which they had been brought. They stood at the side of the massive wall looking upward. Its height was intimidating, and the seepage of the fog had a haunting effect.

"Now what do we do?" Christian asked.

The saint did not speak, but smiled encouragingly at the young teenager. Christian's hand grazed the rope at his side. There was no way it would be long enough...and it had no anchor, but still he wondered, *If this gift allows me to be tethered to divine forces, could it possibly work in making a way for us all to climb over the wall?* He hoped it would, for it would mean they would be able to enter the kingdom in a stealthy manner, without having to break through the walls.

He pulled the rope from his belt and prayed silently. He held the gift up; it dangled from his hand. Suddenly, it began to glow. One end of the rope floated up into the air, its base still resting in the palm of Christian's hand. Up, up, up it rose, and just as Christian thought the rope would surely end, it rose further still.

"It must be growing," he mused.

Higher and higher, it shot up, until finally it whipped to a halt. Christian couldn't see where it had attached itself, but as he pulled sharply on the end in his hand, he found it to be completely secure. "Oh, that's so cool," he whispered. He immediately began to climb up. The rope welcomed his grip. He found the sensation heavenly and not at all like what one would experience using a regular rope. It was as though the rope itself were lifting the boy, and equipped with his footwear, he found the climb exhilarating.

He swiftly traveled up two-thirds of the way, before he noticed the creepy, dark vines gliding over the bulging stones just to his side. He kicked at them, but they continued to worm their way in his direction, easily wrapping themselves over his arms and legs. Thorns punctured his tunic and scratched along his flesh as the vines encircled his chest and began to tighten.

Christian couldn't help panicking. He was finding it difficult to breathe.

Just as he started to feel dizzy and faint, he saw a hand shooting past him. Mary's sparkling glove caught his eye, as the girl gripped the vine that had begun to bind his neck. The glove throbbed and seemed to shoot an electric current through the veiny tendrils. She smiled authoritatively and scolded the plant. "You were not made for this. You must serve your true creator." The vine immediately loosened its hold on Christian's neck, and seemingly, in its need to atone for the assault on the boy, gathered its less thorny, twined extremities and began to weave and braid itself into a strong but elegant hammock. It gently enwrapped the boy, who was still quite weak and sore from the attack. Christian released his grip of the rope and allowed himself to be cradled by the foliage. The hammock swayed as it carried him to the top of the wall, gently depositing the boy onto its wide rim.

The others used Christian's rope to mount the wall and soon joined him on the thick, stony ledge. Serena ran to Christian's side, ensuring he had recovered. She helped him to his feet and handed him his coiled rope, and then the children all stood, surveying the forbidding formation before them.

The kingdom looked as if it had been designed to be a large labyrinth, a monstrous maze. Sections of the land were blackened and reflected the light of the moon, indicating the presence of long bodies of water. Other areas were saturated with the same opaque, pale-greenish fog that streamed toward the walls, climbing up and over its edges. In those sections of the maze, there was no way of knowing what menaces might be hiding within.

At the very center of the kingdom, there was a dark, twisted mountain. It looked like a dreadfully deformed wasp's nest, looming over the land. Surrounding the hill was a sprawling forest. The trees were bony and spiny, and seemed deprived of life. The branches were furiously fused and reached up to the gnarled nest, where the thick, netted layers surrounding the formation made it difficult to see who or what lay within, but the children sensed that the whole area was alive with hidden, rustling movements.

"This is not good," Joachim said, shaking his head and reaching for Allora's hand. "Why would Kingsley make a kingdom that looks so...ugly?"

Allora shook her head. "I would imagine that this is a fairly good representation of Kingsley's disturbed mind. It's so scary."

"This is wonderful," St. John Henry said suddenly, with a satisfied smile. The children looked at him with puzzled expressions. "Joachim has placed us in the most advantageous position. Do you see the highest point at the center of the kingdom?" The children nodded. "That will be our final destination, but first we must break into groups that will facilitate an expeditious escape for the captives. They are spread out within the labyrinth, with each form of imprisonment unique to its group of prisoners."

He pointed to one of the dark-pooled areas. "Look there. That is where Kingsley has detained the residents who fought hardest against his lies and manipulation. They were the ones with clear, sharp minds who tried to pull others from his grip, and so he has fortified their prisons with riddles and isolation. In his narcissistic existence, he believes his riddles to be unsolvable, as he perceives his level of intelligence to extend beyond mere human capability."

Liam cleared his throat. "I actually really love riddles and would love to be in the group."

"I suspected as much," the saint said grinning. "Christian will join you, and I think Angelica should most assuredly be a part of your company, for she has a dear friend who is being kept there."

"Is it Edward?" Angelica piped up. "He definitely had a clear mind and was trying to let people know that something wasn't right."

"Yes," he replied. "And his wife, Violet, is there as well, but they continue to be separated."

Angelica frowned. "I definitely want to help free them!"

The saint then spoke to Allora and Serena. "Sophia is being kept in the part of Kingsley's kingdom that suppresses the most creative minds and trusting hearts. They are completely bound and guarded by cunning creatures. I am sending you to free her. You will need to make use of your gifts to assure her safe release."

Will looked a little hurt and confused. "She's my great aunt; shouldn't I be the one to rescue her?"

"She is blessed to have you as her nephew. You have filled her life with your love, care, and affirmation. I ask you to offer those same gifts to the ones who have not been so fortunate," he continued.

"You, Mary, and Joachim will release the captives who have been detained in the forest surrounding Kingsley's lair. They were the ones who easily fell prey to him, as they had already been neglected by friends and family. They were alone, in a broken state, believing their lives no longer had value or meaning. They roam the dark forest, easily confined within its borders, for they have no reason to escape. Kingsley demands that they offer him homage and service, and they readily comply. Releasing these particular captives will be more difficult than you think, for they are without hope."

He looked at the three children. "You have so much to offer them, and I believe you will find a way to reveal to them their true worth. Rekindle in them a desire for truth, life, and freedom."

He blessed the children and urged them to use great caution, impressing upon them the importance of not under-estimating their adversary.

CHAPTER 26

Liam, Christian, and Angelica made their way along the rim of the stone wall. They could see the dark water in the distance. St. John Henry Newman had urged them to use their imagination to devise the quickest route to the prisoners. Angelica had something in mind, but wasn't quite sure if her gift would allow it.

"We need to find a way down, and then we can start to work our way through the labyrinth," Liam stated.

Christian sighed heavily. "It may take a while. The river, or whatever it is, is pretty far into the maze, and even with our footwear, there's probably a ton of obstacles that will slow us down."

Angelica cleared her throat loudly, attempting to draw their attention. She then pulled her small rock from its chain and seemed to be concentrating deeply. The rock vibrated and, as she set it on the ground at the lip of the rim, it seemed to crack and grow, altering its shape into a long, thick stone. And then it multiplied. Out of the first, a second gray slab of rock grew, and then more flat rocks appeared, each layering itself upon the last. The light rumbling continued, as the children were caught up in the mesmerizing sight of what looked like the ruffling of stone feathers, gracefully yet speedily extending into the distance, over the divides between the walls. When the noise and movement finally ceased, the children were delighted to discover that a perfect, formidable bridge had been created, forging a path between the wall on which they stood and the inner wall that was closest to the water.

Christian's eyes were bulging as he stared at his little sister in disbelief. He couldn't help feeling a slight tinge of jealously. He took a step out onto the bridge and turned to his sister. "What, you couldn't have imagined up some handrails?" he teased.

Angelica smiled, lifting her chin as she joined her brother on the bridge. "Maybe try imagining up some balance," she quipped. She swiftly ran across the structure, calling out "Try to keep up!" Christian was somewhat amused, but determined not to let the spirited girl beat him to their destination. He quickly moved along the layers of stone, with Liam following closely behind.

. . .

Allora and Serena stood at the edge of the stone wall,

gazing down into the dark abyss below. St. John Henry was right: Joachim had brought them to the perfect spot. They were told that Sophia was being kept just below their feet, imprisoned in a large field between the two outer rings of the labyrinth. They were relieved that they wouldn't have to travel too far, especially since neither Allora's gift nor Serena's would help in expediting their journey.

They carefully climbed down over the side of the rim, holding fast to the edge.

Mary had done them a great service before leaving with Will and Joachim. She had placed her gloved hands on the sprawling vines that covered the inside of the wall and whispered to them. They had responded by weaving and twisting themselves into a long, smooth ladder. As she waved goodbye to the girls, she had assured them of her prayers and they had returned the promise.

Allora was first to descend the ladder. She was nervous, for she couldn't stop thinking about the description of Sophia's prison. The saint had said that the captives were being guarded by cunning creatures and she wasn't sure she wanted to meet them.

"Hurry!" Serena implored her sister in a hushed whisper.

Allora continued her descent. Soon her foot grazed a shoot of wild grass. She jumped from the ladder, landing waist high in sprouts of tall weeds and dry bushes. Serena was soon at her side and the two surveyed the vast field. Though shrouded in darkness, lit only by a hint of the moon's glow, they could tell that the field stretched quite far along the alley of the maze.

"I wonder where the prisoners are being held," Allora whispered. She was grateful that their blessed footwear silenced their steps, for she felt the dry twigs threatening to snap beneath her feet and she did not want to alert anyone, be it friend or foe, to their presence.

"Look," Serena whispered, pointing to white, rounded patches of cottony flowers. "I've never seen anything like that before."

Allora examined the beautiful, domed, fluffy batches. They were considerable: one deposit would easily fill a large wheelbarrow, and there were quite a few of them.

Allora smiled and quietly mused, "I think I remember seeing these flowers in Sophia's drawings. They're so lovely." She reached out her hand and stroked the soft, fluttery petals. They felt like down feathers. Suddenly the cluster moved. Allora jumped back. She spun around, inspecting each patch, and could tell that they were all moving. It was almost as though they were grazing.

"Maybe they're sheep... or something like that. They seem pretty harmless," Serena said quietly. "I actually think they're kind of cute."

Allora sighed. "You may be right, but everything in this kingdom makes me nervous."

They continued through the narrow meadow, walking close to the wall, and as they curved around, they soon

made out a few tall trees in the distance. Dangling from the trees were huge pods. As the girls got closer, they could see that inside each pod was a silhouette: a shadowy occupant. Serena froze. "Okay, now I'm nervous."

Allora crouched down and quickly pulled her sister down beside her. She squinted, trying to make out the figures. "Come on," she whispered. "We need to get closer, so we can get a better view." The two girls moved slowly, cautiously creeping, their hearts beating a little faster as they approached the trees.

One of the fluffy domed critters nudged Allora in a comforting gesture. She placed her hand on its furry petals before forging on. The creature moved more quickly, placing itself directly in her path, blocking her way. "Are you trying to protect us?" she whispered. "It's okay, we'll be fine." The furry ball quivered its petals, making it clear that it did not want the girls to go any closer to the pods.

Allora backed up a bit and surveyed the area. Was there a way to go around the trees? Were the shadows in the pods aware of their presence? Serena looked over at her sister, "Why did we stop?" she quietly asked.

"I think we need to take a moment to consider our options," Allora responded.

"Maybe we should take a moment to pray too," Serena whispered, as she grasped the heart-shaped ruby around her neck. She bowed her head, praying silently. The heart began to glow, and she was surprised as words began to pour from her lips, almost outside her control. It was the Prayer of St. Michael. Allora joined her sister in prayer.

"*St. Michael the Archangel, defend us in battle.*

Be our defense against the wickedness and snares of the Devil.

May God rebuke him, we humbly pray, and do thou,

O Prince of the heavenly hosts, by the power of God,

thrust into hell Satan, and all the evil spirits,

who prowl about the world seeking the ruin of souls. Amen."

As they finished the prayer, they noticed that the flowery fur balls seemed to be quivering more frantically. "Look," Serena whispered, her face directed to the sky. A small flicker of light was dancing just above them. It grew larger, until it had become a golden, translucent, flaming heart. It descended down before Allora until it rested just above her locket.

"Of course," Allora whispered. "We need the light of understanding."

She opened her locket. It now acted as a pure light, illuminating the field. She focused the gentle beam on one of the pods suspended from a tree. The light caused the pod to glow and Allora gasped, as she saw the clearly defined face of a child, who looked to be about eleven years old, staring out in her direction. Her hands were clenching thick, knotted bars made from the branches extending from the tree. Allora could now see that the pods were really suspended cages, meant to hold Kingsley's captives. The young prisoner was wearing a white gown and she had long blonde hair and somewhat familiar eyes.

"Sophia?" Allora pondered out loud. "Could it be?"

Allora then turned the beam on the floral, sheep-like critter that was still in her path. "Oh no," she whispered. The light seemed to penetrate through its cottony exterior, revealing something strange and grotesque within.

She jumped back, bumping into her sister. They both watched, horrified as the white bundle slowly split down the middle and a black, hairless creature emerged.

Serena screamed, and Allora protectively wrapped her arms around the small girl.

The creature looked like a wolf but more slick and beastly. It flashed its teeth and growled, lowering its head as though preparing to pounce.

The gold light that had descended on Allora rose up between them. It seemed to fan out, transforming into a huge, magnificent shield.

The sisters tucked themselves under its mantle. It responded in turn by wrapping itself around them, creating a perfect, impenetrable bubble. The snarling beasts were seething. There were six of them, and they paced back and forth, their eyes alive with rage. Growing impatient, one of the creatures lunged viciously at the shield. It yelped as it was zapped: a surge of electric gold light fusing through its body before the beast seemed to fizzle away. A black, woeful, shadowy figure remained momentarily before vanishing completely.

The other slimy beasts howled in protest. One of the creatures, who was much larger than the rest, calmly walked over and positioned himself an inch from the shield. He seemed to look deeply and threateningly into Allora's eyes before turning his attention to Sophia. He glanced one last time at Allora, with what she perceived to be a taunting expression of imminent triumph, before dashing at full speed in the prisoner's direction. The other creatures followed suit, growling and snapping as they dashed toward the captives. The pods were shaking, as the frantic, fearful children clawed at the twined bars.

"No!" Allora cried out. "Leave them alone!"

She turned to her sister, urgently pleading, "What can we do to stop them from attacking the prisoners?!"

Serena looked determined. She grasped her pendant once more, and lowered her head in prayer. The ruby glowed and Serena's voice rose confidently. "Allora, hold up your light, and shine it in the direction of the children."

Allora followed her instructions. Serena held up the stone of piety into the path of the beam. The light became a red stream expanding to cover each of the prisoners. Serena spoke the words given to her through her gift of piety:

"ANIMA CHRISTI

Soul of Christ, sanctify me. Body of Christ, save me. Blood of Christ, inebriate me. Water from the side of Christ, wash me. Passion of Christ, strengthen me. O good Jesus, hear me. Within thy wounds hide me. Separated from thee let me never be. From the malignant enemy, defend me. At the hour of death, call me. And close to thee bid me. That with thy saints I may be praising thee, forever and ever. Amen."

The rabid, black animals, who had also been caught in the light, shrieked as though singed from the flow of prayer. Smoke rose from the points of contact as the wounded creatures' bodies tightened into slimy coils before dissipating. Five shadowy figures, wretched and weak, remained for a moment before evaporating into the moist air.

The children in the cages stood awestruck. They gripped the bars once more but found them to be brittle, having been sapped of strength by the powerful stream of graces. The prisoners burst out of their confines and ran excitedly to the sisters. The child, who Allora was now sure must be Sophia, stared at the girls, tearing up with gratitude. She didn't speak a word, but placed a hand over her heart and smiled deeply, before fading away. All of the children followed, wispily dancing as mist in the air before disappearing completely.

Allora gasped. "Do you think she's okay?"

Serena nodded. "I think she's free now, and I think Pam will be so happy to finally have her sister back."

CHAPTER 27

"It's a long way down," Angelica said, as she looked over the edge to the body of water below. Liam adjusted his glasses before scanning the area. "There looks to be about four feet of land running along the wall. We just need to find a way down."

"I guess you'll be needing my rope," Christian submitted. Angelica raised an eyebrow. "You know I could just make a huge staircase, right?" Christian frowned slightly. "My gift is a little quieter than yours, hence more stealthy, hence probably the better option," he stated.

"You have the loudest voice, hence lowering the chances of any kind of stealthy entrance," she whispered. Christian frowned more deeply, and Angelica sighed. "Sorry, I know you're right. We should use your rope. My gift is pretty loud." She smiled mischievously, adding "because it's so powerful." She giggled as her brother playfully shoved into her.

He approached the edge of the wall and held out the golden rope. One end floated up slightly, before diving down into the valley below. After it seemed to have reached its destination, the other end, still cupped in Christian's hand, broke free and burrowed itself into the rocky ledge beneath his feet. Christian reached down and gave the rope a strong tug. Once again, he found it to be completely secure.

The children descended one by one, with Christian leading the way. When they had all landed on the firm ground, Christian gently tugged the rope. It readily released its grip on the rim and, in a mystical manner, slowly floated down to the boy. He coiled it over his hand before attaching it at his waist.

"This looks really dreary," Angelica slowly whispered, her words lingering, as foggy breath carried over the waters. It was difficult to see anything. "How do we know which way we should go?"

Christian pointed down the river to an area that was thick with a strange, diaphanous mist. "I think I see something way down there," he whispered. "It looks like it could be people on rafts. We should definitely go that way."

"Wait," Liam urged. He agreed with his brother. It did appear to be prisoners, but he had to sure. He reached into his shirt and pulled out the monocle attached to the chain. He held up the precious item. It glowed slightly as he looked through to the figures down the river. "Nope!" he said suddenly, in an urgent whisper. "Duck down!"

Through the glass, he could see that the figures were

really dark, slimy beasts, pacing along a shallow section of water on small mounds of earth and twisted, black logs.

"I think it best we go in the opposite direction."

Christian, who had also glanced through the glass, nodded slowly, his skin suddenly a shade paler.

"Do you think they saw us?" he asked.

"They're not heading in our direction, so I think we might safe...for now," Liam answered.

The group quietly made their way up the river. They came upon a small bridge spanning the width of the water. It looked as though it had grown up out of the riverbed. Six trees, dark and wet, with twisted, interlocking branches formed the eerily knotted structure.

Angelica looked to her older brother. "Should we cross it? Is it safe?"

Liam grasped his monocle. "Negative," he whispered. "It appears intact, but it's just an illusion. The end trees and a few feet of the bridge are solid, but that's it. There's a wide gap, hidden by a large span of twisted planks... or rather the image of twisted planks. There's nothing there." He lowered the monocle.

Christian grunted. "I really don't like this place."

Angelica looked confused. "Would it really be such a big deal if we fell in the water? We're all strong swimmers."

Liam shook his head. "I saw something else through the glass. You're not going to like it. Look." He held up the monocle, allowing his siblings to see into the river surrounding the bridge. Angelica gasped as the glass became a window to the world under the waters. Huge, vile creatures swam menacingly. There were a multitude of them filling the spaces below. Seeing their piranha-like jaws, eel-like tails, and strange thin tentacles, the children unanimously agreed that swimming would never be an option.

"We need to stay on the path," Liam said decidedly.

The siblings continued along the side of the river, glancing back every few seconds to ensure they weren't being followed by any unwanted companions. Soon they came to an area filled with the sound of creaking wood, clinking chains, and wet movement. It was quite dark, but they could make out shapes in the middle of the river. As they got closer, they could see several small rafts, more like broken planks of wood, floating randomly about. Each carried a small child dressed in tattered peasants' robes. They were chained to the platforms, and each raft seemed anchored in place. They bore fragmented words and verses that had been painted in white, grotesque strokes.

"What does the writing mean?" Angelica asked Liam, knowing that he was the most likely to recognize the random scrawls.

"I'll admit I'm a little confused," he answered. "They seem to be verses and passages from Scripture, but they're mixed up between the rafts. It's like they're not in their proper place or context, which makes it very difficult to properly decipher their true meaning."

The water was quite still about the rafts, save for the slightest movement of broken twigs moving down the river, indicating the presence of a gentle current. The children upon the wooden planks were lying with their knees tucked into their chests.

"Are they real?" Angelica whispered to her brother.

Liam raised his small glass and nodded. "It's not an illusion."

The imprisoned children soon became aware of the presence of visitors and stood, holding up their hands frantically, as though warning them not to enter the water. One of the children, a girl with ebony hair, slipped on the wet board as she was motioning and fell hard on the raft. It wavered, and her foot lightly grazed the water. Within a moment, a large set of fangs cut through the surface, thrashing in her direction. She quickly pulled her feet back, hugging her knees and burying her face. The creature disappeared.

"Poor things," Angelica whispered. "What a horrible place to be trapped. How do we free them?" She thought for a moment. "I could make a rock bridge to get to them, maybe."

Liam again consulted his monocle and shook his head in frustration. "The chains are around their necks and they go through the middle of the rafts and down about ten feet through the water, where they seem to be embedded in the bedrock beneath." He sighed. "So even if you make a bridge, we wouldn't be able to pull them from the rafts." Angelica wrinkled her brow, deep in thought, before admitting that she couldn't think of a solution. The chains were probably too thick to break, even with her rock, and she acknowledged that attempting to smash them would mean putting the wet, rotten-looking panels of wood at risk of breaking, exposing the children to the aquatic monsters beneath.

"So, what can we do?" she asked. "How do we rescue them?"

"By solving the riddles," Liam answered. He was busy looking through his monocle.

"What riddles?" she said, squinting her eyes, as she surveyed the area. "Do you mean the writing on the rafts?"

"Actually, I think we should start with this one," he replied, motioning to a large rock that was exposed at the river's edge. Christian inspected the rock carefully. "It's just a rock. A very dirty rock."

"Wipe it off," Liam instructed. "There's an inscription under the mud."

Christian bent over and rubbed the rock's surface. Soon, words were visible. He cleared his throat and read aloud. "I am four, but half of me is five." Christian stood up and crossed his arms over his chest, shaking his head. "Half of four is two, not five."

Angelica placed her hands on her hips and started tapping her foot, as though it would somehow help stir up her thoughts. "I wish I could hang upside down. I think better that way," she huffed. "Wait, what if it's the shape of the number four. Is there a way to split it in half so that it looks like the number five?"

Liam was scanning the area while contemplating the riddle. He stopped suddenly and smiled excitedly. "I've got it," he said confidently. He walked over to the section of the wall that was closest to the rock bearing the riddle and pointed to a large fracture in one of the flat stones embedded on the wall's surface.

"It looks like a V," Angelica commented, slightly confused at her brother's enthusiasm.

"It's the Roman numeral for five. The Roman numeral for four consists of two shapes: a vertical line and then a V, so if you split the two, half of the four is actually a V: the number five."

Christian looked very impressed for a second, and then was quickly overcome by his impulsive nature. "I'm pushing it," he stated, as he lunged at the stone, pressing with all of his might. The stone easily sank further into the wall and the path beneath Christian's feet suddenly dropped open. The tall teenager dropped into a pit, rolling down a few steps made of hardened dirt and dried clay. "Ouch!"

Angelica and Liam peered over the side. "Are you okay?" Liam inquired. "Yeah," Christian said quietly, still stunned from the fall. He got up and dusted off his tunic as he tried to scan the area.

Angelica skipped down the steps. "It's pretty dark in here, but there's a torch we can light. Liam, a little help?"

Liam proudly produced his lighter and lit the torch. There were six steps leading down from the surface, then a small landing. The next set of stairs curved around in the direction of the water. There were about twelve steps leading down to a tunnel that seemed to run under the river.

The children walked slowly, carefully examining the walls of the tunnel, searching for some indication of their next riddle. Finally, they came to an area that was assuredly the middle of the river, directly under the children's rafts. The tunnel had widened vastly, so that it was more like a large cavern. They could hear the sound of dripping and as they inspected the ceiling, they found the bottom section of the prisoner's chains locked into place.

"So we need to figure out a way to release the chains," Angelica surmised. "But how?"

Liam, who was looking through his monocle, was smiling again.

"By solving another riddle, of course."

CHAPTER 28

Will, Mary, and Joachim were closing in on the inner layer of the labyrinth. Mary's gift had proven to be extremely useful. At each stony rim she had stopped to remind the vines of their true Creator, and they had responded in service, by fashioning themselves into steadfast suspension bridges. Joachim was a little nervous to cross over them at first, for they swayed and creaked with the motion, but he soon found his courage and mastered the feat.

"Okay," Mary whispered. "Time to descend into the creepy, freaky forest surrounding Kingsley's horrifying and probably demon-infested lair." Joachim frowned. "Do you really need to describe it that way?"

Mary shrugged. "I'm compelled to speak the truth."

The three made their way down the wall and into the valley below. The area was thick with sharp, twined trees and underbrush. Will frowned. "What a mess. How do we even begin to make our way through this? I'm kind of wishing Allora was here to blast a path for us."

Mary smiled. "I think we'll be fine. I just have to remind this forest of who it should really be serving." She then added teasingly, "But I'm guessing that that's not the only reason you wish Allora was here." Even in the dim light, Mary could tell Will was blushing. Joachim looked a little confused. "What's going on here? Why are we talking about Allora?"

"Never mind," Mary sang, as she gripped the branches and vines just in front of her. Her gloves throbbed, fusing the tangled masses with light and vibration. Slowly the trees and bushes rose into an archway. It was an exciting, magnificent sight. The constant winding movement was mesmerizing, as was the creaking, snapping, rustling, and cracking that filled the air. In the end, a majestic, lacy, organic tunnel lay before them. It seemed to be leading the children in the direction of the lair.

. . .

Angelica scanned the walls. "Where do you see a riddle?" she asked her brother.

"It's on the wall just behind us," Liam replied. "I can see it through my monocle, but my sense is that it can usually only be seen in the darkness, which would be the usual state of this tunnel."

He extinguished the torch and sure enough, letters became visible on one of the walls.

"Call me a scuttling crustacean,

A lasting verdancy.

I am the residue of fire,

I ache for love.

I lie in your hand."

"Hmmm, tricky," Angelica said, as she searched her mind.

Liam was deep in thought. He shook his head. "I think we should take it line by line."

Angelica wrinkled her brow. "What's a crustacean?"

"It's an ocean creature, like a lobster or crab. The scuttling seems to describe a crab."

"And what does verdancy mean?" she asked.

"It means the color green," Liam stated. "A lasting green."

Christian perked up. "Recycling!" he called out.

Liam frowned. "I can't see Kingsley writing a riddle involving recycling."

Angelica gasped excitedly. "I think I know it. A lasting green could be an evergreen."

"I think the residue of fire is pretty straightforward: ash," Liam submitted. "But the ache for love is a little unclear."

Angelica walked over to a wall and bent over, tying her dress through the middle, converting it into pants.

"What are you doing?" Christian asked.

She then proceeded to do a handstand against the wall's surface.

"I need to be upside down," she announced. "It helps me think better."

Liam was pacing. "What does it mean to ache for love?"

"To yearn?" Christian suggested.

"To desire?" Angelica added.

"Or," Liam mused, "perhaps to pine."

"UGH!" Angelica fell down from her stance. She stood up and rubbed her hands together. "My palms were getting sore."

Just then she jumped up and down excitedly. The motion released the fabric of her gown into a dress once more.

Liam raised an eyebrow. Angelica held up her hand. "I have the answer to the last line... I think. I lie in your hand: PALM!"

Liam adjusted his glasses. "So we have: crab, evergreen, ash, not totally sure about the fourth line, and palm."

All three siblings looked at each other and unanimously spoke. "Trees"

"So, I guess the fourth one was pine—another type of tree," Christian said proudly.

Angelica scanned the wall and yelped when she noticed a fissure that clearly resembled an intricate tree. It was etched into a large, flat stone.

"I'm gonna press the stone this time," Angelica stated. She reached out and pressed her hands on the image but was careful to jump to the side, just in case a pit were to appear. But there was no pit; instead, pressing on the stone seemed to cause something to unhinge, and the rock's flat surface dropped open as a flap, revealing a panel on the wall behind it.

Above the panel of letters, there was yet another riddle:

"I have a bed, but never sleep,

I have a mouth, but never talk.

I will rush, but will not leap.

I'm always running, though I can't walk."

Liam adjusted his glasses and looked up, in thought. He wondered aloud, "A bed...flowers have a bed, but don't sleep. However, they can't run. What can rush and run, but not leap or walk?"

Christian piped up, "Water!"

"Yes," Liam agreed. "Water—but a body of water that has a bed and mouth, and is always running..."

"A river!" Angelica cried out.

"Exactly," Liam said. "Try River."

Angelica pressed the letters and as soon as she had pushed the final button, the large pieces of metal binding the great chains to the ceiling dropped open. It only took a moment for the chains to begin sliding back up through the holes, and slowly, water began to trickle through the open voids.

"Let's not stay in here," Angelica suggested, her eyes fixed on the water now streaming into the tunnel.

The children ran up the stairs, rushing to the river's edge. The small prisoners stood, looking both confused and amazed as they slowly pulled the chains up through the middle of the rafts.

"Look!" Angelica exclaimed, as she pointed to the planks of wood that were now beginning to move down the river.

"Can I build a bridge now?" she asked her brother.

"I think that would be good idea," Christian replied in earnest. "Otherwise, they'll float right through the fake bridge and into the area where those freakishly ugly beasts are hanging out."

"On it!" Angelica cried, as she ran quickly along the side of the river. It was good that she was such a fast runner, for soon she was about thirty feet ahead of the slow-moving rafts. She bent down, placing her stone just beside the water. "Come, Holy Spirit," she whispered. The stone once again split, vibrating and growing. As if it were aware of the high stakes, the rock seemed to work more quickly this time, multiplying and swiftly skipping over the waters, creating a magnificent, low-lying bridge.

"Come on, guys," she called to her brothers. They soon joined her, and the three children hurried to the middle of the bridge, bending low and extending their hands in anticipation of the children's arrival.

Yelping, snarling, and growling caused the siblings to freeze in terror. Christian slowly turned his head to scan the grounds at the sides of the river. He gasped as he saw the flash of teeth and vile, shadowy figures, furiously dashing in their direction.

"Ohhh noooo," he breathed. Angelica was speechless, her mind racing as her eyes were uncontrollably jetting back and forth. "Where is that courage I'm supposed to have?" she thought to herself. Then she laid her palms flat against the bridge's stony surface. "I've got this," she whispered to herself, before clarifying: "YOU've got this," she whispered in prayer. She closed her eyes and thought of the strength of the One who had entrusted her with this mission. The wolf-like, hairless creatures were almost at either side of the bridge when it suddenly began to rumble. Each end of the structure shot up, as giant, powerful walls. They both grew to at least twelve feet and extended several feet beyond the edges of the bridge.

The animals were maniacally raging and barking at the barriers. Some tried to jump up, but were unable to mount them. They slid down, helplessly scraping and scratching their claws along the stone. There were three creatures on either side. Two from one of the sides tried to weasel their way around the barrier but found themselves slipping into the river. There was great splashing and thrashing as the beasts were quickly snatched up by the river monsters. They disintegrated and their residual black shadows rose above the river before vanishing.

The children, still grasping the chains attached to their necks, were almost at the bridge. The siblings quickly pulled them up onto the stony surface, careful not to let a single extremity touch the water. Angelica noticed that a little boy with red hair was especially protective of the ebony-haired girl. They seemed to know each other well. She was sure it must be Edward and Violet, for he had told her they had met as children and so would surely recognize each other, even in their youthful state. Her eyes were warm with tears as she saw them hugging, the joy of their reunion almost tangible.

The other children looked at the siblings, relieved to be free of their rafts but still carrying the chains bound at their necks.

"Now, how do we break their chains?" Christian said.

Liam was looking at the words on the fragments of wood. "Maybe there's one last riddle… or perhaps a puzzle." He began scanning the words and sentences as he mused aloud, "Saint John Henry Newman was always appalled by those who would take Scripture, or even his own words, out of context. He found it to be deceptive, divisive, and misleading. I think freeing the prisoners is bound to the text written on their rafts. I think we need to piece them all together and make sure they are placed in the right order."

They examined the words on each ramshackle raft:

And you will know

My disciples

Will set

You are truly

In my word

If you abide

You free

The truth

And the truth

You are truly

"I'm pretty confused," Angelica admitted.

Liam closed his eyes, searching. His lips were moving, as though working his way silently through passages he had memorized. Finally, he stopped and his eyes shot open. He turned to Christian.

"I think we need to use your rope to latch onto the rafts and pull them into the right order." Christian was happy to have a role in solving the puzzle. Liam pointed to one of the planks of wood. "That one goes first. Pull it over all the way to the left of the bridge," he instructed. Then he pointed to another one. "That one's next; it goes beside it." One by one the pieces were selected. Christian simply held his rope in the direction of the chosen raft, and the golden braid would thread itself onto the plank and drag it to its proper place. Once the slabs of wood had all been reordered, Liam declared excitedly, "It's John 8:31–32." The siblings stood together and read out loud.

"If you abide in my word, you are truly my disciples, and you will know the truth, and the truth will set you free."

As soon as the words had passed over their lips, Kingsley's captives lifted their hands to the sky. At the sound of heavy chains dropping, the prisoners began to float above the waters. They were translucent and free, caught up in a heavenly dance. They rose and twirled, as a swirl of gentle light, until they had disappeared completely.

The silence ushered in a peace like no other in the hearts of the siblings, who were still staring into the night sky, swelling with gratitude. "It's done," Christian whispered. The quiet was broken when the slick beasts released deathly howls.

"I had almost forgotten about them," Angelica sighed. "I guess now we just have to rescue ourselves."

"Not a problem," Christian asserted. He walked to the side of the bridge where two of the beasts had fallen victim to the predators in the river. The one remaining creature was standing just to the side of the barrier, crouching low, as though ready to attack. Christian lifted his rope into the air, pointing it at the demonic vermin. The rope whipped out instantaneously, binding the beast's snout and then wrapping itself around his torso. The rope then lifted the creature and dangled it over the waters, before releasing its grip. There was a single splash as the river (and the creatures beneath) swallowed up the animal. A dark, weaselly shadow rose just above the surface before fizzling away.

The other black creatures backed up, as though fearful of the same fate, and scurried off into the distance.

Christian kissed his rope victoriously. "So, that was pretty amazing," he said with a smile. Angelica agreed, but pushed her brother along, saying, "We need to find the others. I'm sure we still have more work to do."

CHAPTER 29

In a small, dingy cave, Kingsley sat upon his throne, guarded by two beasts who stood at his sides.

His mind was racing, sifting through possible courses of action—of retaliation. Here he was safe. Here he was king, and no one could penetrate the crown of his intellect and imaginings.

He stood and proudly strode out through the contorted archway, leading to a balcony made of clay and braided vines. He leaned over the rail, surveying his kingdom.

"What is that?" The stunned whisper poured over his lips, as his eyes focused on the wispy trails of delicate light rising above the fog and disappearing into the space beyond. He could feel a pang of loss with each sighting. He could sense that the shadows and forces that were tasked with securing his once powerful and mighty kingdom were now somehow deteriorating. There was a crippling, an air of weakness. The kingdom itself reflected the shift, with some of the rocks crumbling and sliding down from the highest peaks.

Something was definitely amiss. Someone or something was obviously trying to threaten his dominion. He raised his arm and called out furiously. They would answer his cry. They would find the intruders and enslave them, as all had been enslaved.

. . .

"I think something or someone is watching us," Joachim whispered to his sister, as they walked through the tunnel of twisted trees. Mary squinted, trying to see through the trellis-like branches. Joachim was right. There was definitely movement: a wisp of white through the rustling dry bushes.

"I think it's the children, Kingsley's servants," Will said softly.

"How do you know?" Mary asked.

"They're scared and confused. I can hear them. They don't trust us."

"I don't blame them," Mary said sadly. "I'm sure Kingsley's convinced them that no one really cares about them."

"Guys," Joachim said suddenly. "We're going the wrong way."

"We can't be, the trees are ordered to God's service, so they wouldn't lead us in the wrong direction," Mary insisted.

Joachim held up his compass. "I'm telling you, we're supposed to go that way," he protested, pointing to the side of the tunnel. Mary sighed, defeated. "Fine," she said. "We'll follow your compass."

Will walked over to the branches and began to pull them apart. The trees, still wanting to assist the children, responded to the slightest touch, so Will was easily able to forge a path under Joachim's direction.

"Turn left here, please," the boy instructed his companion. Will continued to sweep away the brush, then stopped suddenly. "I know where your compass is leading us," he said. He pointed to a large, hollowed oak tree that could be seen through the thinning branches and bracken. "Just a few more feet and we should see her," he whispered.

"You must be right," Joachim affirmed. His compass had risen above his hand and begun to spin.

Sure enough, a few short steps led them through the last of the weeds and thinly twined vines and into a small clearing. There was a gaping hole at the base of the knotted tree, and a small girl, whose face looked mature for her slight stature, timidly peaked out from its trunk.

Will pulled out St. John Henry's crest and held it tightly. He looked into the little girl's large brown eyes, which seemed weary and scared, and he spoke from his heart. "We come as friends. Please don't be afraid." She sank back slightly into the tree. Will heard a quiet, sweet voice. It penetrated his thoughts.

"Leave me. I'm no one."

"No," Will thought. "We are here to free you. I'm Will.

What's your name?"

The little girl's head shot back into view. Her eyes were wide, shocked at the exchange.

"How can you hear me?" her heart exclaimed.

"We have been sent, because you are loved. We want to remind you of your life's beauty and purpose."

"My name is Rachel. I am alone. You say my life has purpose. If that's true, why was I left alone?"

"I'm sorry you felt abandoned."

"You shouldn't be here. We're not supposed to get too close to anyone. I'll get in trouble."

"You don't have to stay here. We can help you escape this world."

"And go where? I don't know exactly where I was before, but there remains a lingering trace of feelings from a former life: loneliness, disappointment, and fear of being unloved. I'm somehow aware of having waited, and waited, but having no one come. I don't remember anything else, but those sentiments are enough to tell me that this is where I should remain." The girl looked down, tracing her finger along the trunk of the tree, as tears filled her eyes. "I don't know what happened in that former life, but the feeling of being completely unwanted, that will always stay with me."

Will crouched down and looked sympathetically into Rachel's eyes.

"I can't imagine what you must have experienced, feeling so neglected and unloved. Rachel, I would really love to have known you in that world." He clarified. "I'd really like to have the chance to find you there and to know you more."

"My home is here."

"This place isn't real, and it's keeping you from the hope of something beautiful and true. Please, let us take you back to where you can be seen and cared for. I promise that I will find you outside of this horrible place. Please give me the chance to show you that your life matters. Please, Rachel."

The thin girl slowly emerged from the tree. "I'll travel awhile with you, but I am not ready to leave this place. You don't understand what it was like. I don't want to leave this prison only to return to another." She cautiously made her way to Will, who took her hand. "I meant what I said," he assured her. "It made me happy being able to visit my aunt and show her I cared, even when it seemed like she didn't know I was there. I would really love to be there for you too."

He gently began to lead her back to the path.

"Perhaps," her heart whispered.

"Wait," Mary said. She gestured to the long, dry grass and bushes surrounding the tree.

Will turned to Rachel. "Are there many of you here?" She nodded before turning and beckoning with a gentle wave of her hand. Slowly, many small figures arose from the brittle shrubbery.

"We were instructed to gather dried branches to burn. Our king enjoys seeing a great fire. He says it commemorates the day he was given his freedom and the promise of power."

The young children approached the group but were careful to keep their distance from the visitors as well as each other.

Rachel looked solemnly at Will. "As you can see, there are a great many of us, but we are not allowed to go near each other, and we can't speak. So, even in here, we remain alone."

Will turned to the children. "I hope you can all hear me."

They all looked surprised that his words were able to penetrate their thoughts, though he did not move his lips.

"We were sent here to free you all," he informed the prisoners. "Please, come with us."

The children looked at one another, then lowered their heads and sank back into the dark surroundings.

Mary, though unable to hear Will's plea, understood his attempt to connect with the children. She joined the effort, extending her hand and slowly approaching the children. "Please, don't go," she said softly. She reached out and gently took the hand of a small boy. He jumped slightly, shocked at the contact. "It's okay," she assured him. "We want to help you." He seemed grateful for the warmth of Mary's approach, and the gift of her touch. Something began stirring inside his heart, allowing him to remember a song he once knew. Within the confines of his heart, a hymn surged: *what a friend we have in Jesu*s...He allowed Mary to gently lead him toward the path.

Joachim followed his sister's lead and approached a boy

who looked about his age. "Hi," he said with a kind smile. "I hope you'll let us help you." The boy still looked hesitant.

"Mary," he called to his sister. "Can you touch him with your gloves? Maybe it will help him remember that God loves him."

Mary smiled, approached the boy, and placed her hand delicately on his shoulder.

Just then, she was overcome by ear-piercing shrieks coming from a dark cloud of ravenous, black-winged beings, only a few feet above the oak tree. "Everyone get down!" Will ordered. Mary glanced at the children, who were frozen in fear. "It's okay!" she cried out. "I'll protect you!" She lunged in their direction, attempting to shield them with her body. Immediately, she felt herself swept up. Hundreds of sharp claws clasped her gown at the back and as she cleared the hair that had poured over her face, she soon realized that she was flying high above the tips of the tree. She screamed, wriggling and kicking, as the wretched beasts soared higher and further from her friends. She reached around and managed to grab one of the smaller creatures. She recognized it from a previous spiritual battle. It was a scathe: an incarnate display of pure evil. Her glove sent a pulse into the bat-like creature, and he burst into a puff of black smoke.

"You're all in trouble!" Mary called out in a threatening voice. She reached behind her back, and grabbed at a scathe whose claws were scratching her back. A simple squeeze of the vermin and he puffed away. She reached further back and grasped her next victim. One by one, she attacked the scathes, vaporizing them upon contact.

She was feeling pretty good, until she realized that she was sinking down with each extermination! Soon she was in a free fall, heading directly into a section of the maze that was saturated with the thick, pale-green mist.

With a thud, she hit a small patch of hardened soil and rolled over several times. "OWW!" she groaned as she sat rubbing her sore arm and shoulder. Her dress was smeared with dirt and torn from the scathes' attack. She slowly stood and breathed deeply, fighting off tears as she realized she was completely lost and utterly alone.

CHAPTER 30

"Hello?!" Mary called out. There was an echo, but no indication of where her voice had traveled, for the thickness of the fog prevented her from seeing more than a few feet in any direction. She inspected the small island on which she had been deposited. It was no bigger than a large sandbox. It was devoid of any life, and its edges sloped down into dark, murky waters. Mary waved her arms, attempting to fan away the opaque mist, but to no avail. Even the moon had become her enemy, hiding behind a cloud and depriving her of the slightest hint of light. It was eerily quiet, and Mary couldn't remember the last time she had felt so scared and alone.

She looked down at her gloves, but their former glow had faded. They had been such a great help to her up to this point, but now she would trade them in a heartbeat for Joachim's compass, Angelica's stone, or Allora's light.

She crept close to the edge of her tiny islet, and in spite of the darkness, was able to make out a rock protruding from the water, only a couple feet away. It looked large enough to hold her. Excited at the prospect of going anywhere, she reached her foot out over the water and attempted to step onto the small surface. But just as she began to press the tip of her boot onto its edge, she felt her foot slipping through the object, like a sword cutting through mist. Her foot grazed the water and within a moment, a massive set of arrow-like jaws erupted through the surface and came within inches of sinking its teeth into her leg.

Mary screamed as she fell back onto the island. She scurried to its center, terrified of going anywhere near the edges. She waited and once again, all was silent.

Eventually, she summoned her courage and stood once more. *There must be a way out of here,* she thought to herself. She decided to scan the entire area around her scrap of land—or at least the two feet within the perimeter that would be visible. After walking along the island's edge, she had discovered several rocks similar to the one that had proven to be one of Kingsley's illusions. She wanted desperately to determine if any of them were real, but was definitely not willing to chance losing a limb to whatever creature was lurking in the water. *Now I wish I had Liam's gift*, she sighed, feeling deflated.

She sank down onto the desolate patch, tucking her knees close to her chest. She hung her head and finally

allowed the tears to flow. Her shoulders shook as she felt any hope slipping away.

Just then something broke through the silence. A high, sweet, soaring note. It seemed to pierce through the fog. She reached out her hand, as though somehow she believed she could grab it and draw it in as balm for her weary soul. Then another note penetrated the air, and another. The seraphic sound lifted the child to her feet. "I know this," she whispered. "I've heard this before." The memories of St. John Henry's heavenly hymn filled her heart. She happily imagined the saint somewhere off in the distance calling to her through the outpouring of the divine melody.

Mary had always had a special gift when it came to music. Hearing a song even once allowed her to commit its lyrics to memory. And now the words began to flow from her lips:

"Lead, Kindly Light, amid the encircling gloom, Lead thou me on! The night is dark, and I am far from home, Lead thou me on! Keep thou my feet; I do not ask to see the distant scene; one step is enough for me."

She sighed. "This is everything right now," she mused.

She felt herself being drawn in the direction of the music. She came to the edge of the water and stared at the stone directly in front of her. "One step is enough for me," she whispered.

A thin shimmer of light seemed to dance across the stone. "Thank you, Lord," she said, as she took a deep breath and stepped out onto the rock. She breathed a sigh of relief as she felt the strength and grip of the rock's surface. She looked ahead and saw two large, flat stones. Both lay in the direction of the violin's soothing melody, but she wasn't certain which would prove secure. "Please, Lord, one step." A trickle of light hit the surface to the left, and she happily jumped in its direction. Mary's heart was aflame, for though she could still not yet see the end of her path, she was certain each step would be revealed as she came to it, and it was so.

Finally, she came to the edge of the water and found her dear friend holding his violin and beaming at her. "I am so proud of your courage and your trust, even in the midst of your experience of total abandonment. Well done, my child; well done indeed."

Mary looked down, slightly ashamed. "I may have cried a little," she admitted. "And I was ready to give up."

"Believe me," the saint said in earnest, "there is no shame in crying. It is a beautiful and commendable thing to recognize and acknowledge our weakness, for it is in those moments that we can fully appreciate the power of God and thus offer him our full, undiluted trust. He loves when we turn to him as little children looking to be lifted up."

He smiled reassuringly. "Now, we must join your siblings and the stray souls who are still lingering in Kingsley's grasp. It is time to face the tyrant king directly, and put an end to his depraved domain."

. . .

"Shouldn't we look for your sister?" Will asked the small boy who had drawn the company back to the tunnel of trees.

"My compass is telling me to go this way," Joachim answered. "Maybe it will lead us to Mary."

"Maybe," Will admitted.

"Or maybe it will lead you to your favorite sister!" It was Angelica. She had broken through the side of the tunnel and was looking very proud of herself.

She was followed by Christian and Liam. "So..." she cooed, "we solved a riddle, found a secret tunnel, managed to solve more (near-impossible) riddles, which unlocked the chains binding floating prisoners, built a rock bridge, outsmarted raging, hairless beasts, and cracked a puzzle, freeing the hostages and saving the day!" She smiled triumphantly. "How was your mission?"

Joachim frowned. "It's not a competition." Then his eyes widened. "But Mary did get carried off by creepy bat-like creatures, and now we're hoping we'll be able to find her."

Angelica's smile was gone. "Oh no! Sounds like scathes. I remember those things." She looked scared but determined. "We'll find her," she assured her brother.

"Find who?" a voice called from behind them. The group turned around and saw Allora and Serena running along the path trying to catch up. Their cheeks were red with excitement.

"We were able to release the prisoners at the edge of the labyrinth!" Serena exclaimed. Allora turned to Will. "Your aunt was there," she smiled warmly. "She's free now."

Will hugged Allora but quickly released her, looking a little embarrassed by his impulsive gesture. "That's such a relief. Thank you," he said, his eyes conveying deep gratitude. Allora smiled but looked away quickly, finding his gaze was making her cheeks even redder.

"We should thank Mary," Serena submitted. "We used her

suspension bridges to get here. They're amazing!"

"Why thank you!"

Everyone turned to see Mary parading down the pathway, accompanied by St. John Henry.

"Mary!" Joachim called out excitedly. "How did you..."

The saint raised his hand to the young boy. "We will share stories of our adventures after we defeat our foe," he said with an encouraging smile. "We do not have time to linger in the sweet bliss of reunion. We must thrust ourselves into the marrow of the mission, and we are fast approaching a most crucial encounter. You will be tried, but by God's grace, you will find the true path."

. . .

Kingsley was pacing on his balcony. He knew his kingdom was in danger. They would be coming for him, but he had one last defense, one more trap sure to ensnare any intruder; one more illusion to confound even the wisest would-be infiltrator.

He stood looking to the edge the forest surrounding his lair. A tall figure appeared in the distance, and then another, and yet another. Soon, he could make out a sizable group, approaching his lair with unsettling determination. He squinted and soon was in no doubt of the identity of the trespassers. He froze, as a deer caught in a beam of light. "No," he whispered. It was that priest, and the pesky nieces and nephews. It made no sense. How could they have entered his world? No matter. He drew back into his enclave. He would make sure they would not be leaving.

Two hairless, slimy beasts joined him on the balcony. "Go," he commanded. "Join the others."

CHAPTER 31

"We will once again be separating our happy party, as we have two distinct and important tasks to which we must rise: two parts to our final battle. If successful, we will accomplish Our Lord's most holy will," St. John Henry informed the children.

"Christian, Mary, and Joachim, you will find Kingsley and confront him."

"Ummm..." Mary stammered, "Are you sure we should be facing him alone?"

"You are never alone," the saint replied. "You know this to be true."

"I do," she admitted.

"What about the rest of us?" Allora inquired.

The saint pointed to the top of the nested peaks on Kingsley's mountain. "You must rise to the highest point possible. A blessing is to be poured out over the souls that are still held by Kingsley's lies. You must work together to find a way to ensure that not a single soul is neglected."

"On it!" Angelica said, with a determined nod. St. John Henry pointed to a section just beyond the group, where the ground was beginning to rise.

"This way!" he called out, motioning to an entanglement of trees. Mary hurried to his side. "Let me help you out," she said, reaching down and gripping a mass of the resilient brush. The effect was a rippling of roots and branches, ripping apart and revealing a set of worn-looking steps.

Will turned to the children who had followed the group. "Are you coming?" he asked them. They shook their heads. Rachel looked scared. "We'll stay here."

Will sighed, but understood that they were still struggling to trust. He joined the others and began to mount the stairs.

The saint pointed to another passage leading up another hill. "And there lies your path. Do not allow fear to grip your heart. For all his horrendous acts against the vulnerable, Kingsley remains a man in need of a Savior. And no one is beyond God's mercy."

Christian and Mary nodded. Christian stepped forward and in his deep action-hero voice said, "I'll lead."

"Ahem!" Joachim cleared his throat in protest. He held up his compass. "Would you like to know the best way there?" Christian grunted his consent.

The three set off. Then St. John Henry departed as the

others continued to climb the stone steps.

The narrow steps forced the group to travel in sets of two. Liam led with Angelica at his side. Allora and Serena were next, with Will volunteering to take up the rear. He wanted to make sure no one—or no *thing*—would be sneaking up from behind.

The climb was fairly gradual at first, but then the steps became steeper, more crooked, and much more treacherous.

"It would be nice to have Christian with us," Angelica commented, hardly believing her own words, as he was the one who challenged her patience the most. "Yes," agreed Liam. "His rope would have added some much-needed security to these steps."

With almost perfect timing, Allora's foot caught on a broken section of stone, and she gasped as she started to fall backwards. Will's hands were quickly about her waist, steadying her. She turned her head and said, "Thank you," as he helped her regain her balance. She chastised herself for not having been more careful, but was also not completely regretting the outcome.

"I think that if we hadn't been given our blessed footwear, we would all have fallen down by now," Serena commented. Finally, after mounting a set of particularly steep, wonky steps (more like a stone ladder), they came to a large platform. Standing together, they all smiled, overcome by a great sense of relief, for the next section of the climb boasted a great, elaborate, regal staircase, complete with sturdy yet elegant rails.

At the top, they could make out a lovely cove of heavenly trees, warmed by a soft, entrancing light. "How can something so beautiful exist in Kingsley's world?" Allora mused.

"Well," Will submitted, "the minds that Kingsley pulled into this world are all beautiful. Maybe he's trapped someone especially good and beautiful up there."

"Well," Angelica asserted, "there's only one way to find out!" She dashed toward the staircase but then stopped short. She thought for a moment. "Does anyone else feel like this isn't right?" She sighed, looking longingly at the cove above. "As much as I'd love to head into that lovely light, it doesn't make sense that it's so easily within our reach. Our journey here has been filled with offerings, sacrifices, prayers, and a spirit of selflessness and courage in the face of terrifying obstacles."

Liam stood at Angelica's side. "I think you're right," he admitted. "Saint John Henry Newman made it clear that we have one last battle. That enchanting sight up there seems out of place somehow." He lifted his monocle up and inspected the area. He nodded, saying, "It IS out of place. It's not even there." He motioned for the others to come and see for themselves. The staircase was a grand illusion. It was covering a deep, dark drop. There were gigantic spears at its base, which were aflame with a fire that was somehow void of any light, but fuming with intense heat. Beyond the illusionary staircase, there was simply nothingness. Turning their eyes across a great divide, they saw another, smaller section of the nest-like mountain.

"We should probably head over there," Allora advised. "Saint John Henry said we would need to rise to the highest point possible."

"But I don't see any pathway," Angelica said. "All I see is lots of dark, thorny bushes, and we don't even have Joachim to guide us."

There was a sweet, reddish-orange glow coming from Serena's hands. They were wrapped tightly around her heart-shaped gem, and her lips were moving quickly in a silent prayer.

She looked up as she released her pendant. "We don't need to follow Joa," she stated. Her eyes fell on an area off to the side of the stoned platform, where the thorny bushes were most dense. The children stood with their mouths open, held in a moment of fear and awe. The sound of twigs cracking, of branches creaking and shifting, matched the heaving movement of a massive mound of gnarled vines. There was the distinct moan of labored breath as the silhouette of a man grew out of the thorny tangle. He remained hunched over, the thorns still enshrined densely atop his head. A thick tree with its branches extended as arms, shooting forth from either side, was pressed heavily upon his back, but the figure continued to rise, pulling the tree with awesome passion, prying it from its roots.

He moved along, breaking through jagged, barbed shoots that scraped at his sides.

"He's forging a path for us," Liam said, wonderstruck. "He's making a way."

Serena shook her head and gently whispered, "He IS the way."

She began to follow the figure. Spear-like shards of broken branches struck at her legs. She winced at the sting, but was determined to follow in His path. The others followed suit. The figure began to make his way up a sharp incline of stony steps, and the children were soon aware of the presence of dark, beastly animals at either side of the forged path. They snapped and snarled at the figure and his followers, but he stayed the course, ignoring the vermin. The creatures were growing in number. It was as though every demon in the land had been summoned to this place, to this moment. The depraved predators seem prohibited from fully attacking the group, but that didn't stop them from howling and growling, foaming and frothing, sending sickening huffs of wet, hot breath in their direction.

Some of the children thought about using their gifts to block out the horrid sight or to annihilate the foul creatures, but the figure seemed to accept the persecution and somehow, the children knew they were being called to do the same.

Finally they arrived on even ground atop the hill. The man, still looking more like a darkened silhouette, turned to face the children. He remained bound to the tree he had carried on his back. The trunk of the tree dug at the ground, extending its roots as anchors. It rose up mightily before them, drawing the figure up with it. The motion was quick and focused, alive with twining movement. The cracking and snapping made the sight dismaying, as the figure was contorting and flinching, seemingly in great pain. Then all motion ceased. There remained a solid, unmoving cross. The hairless beasts fell silent.

Out of the stillness and quiet, a great wind suddenly shot forth from the powerful structure. The children bent down low, tucking their faces into the earth and gripping at the soil, while the demonic creatures wailed in high-pitched screeches before turning to dust.

The wind subsided. The children slowly rose to their feet, and Serena surveyed the cross.

"This is where we accomplish our task."

CHAPTER 32

"What is that smell?!"

Kingsley wrinkled his nose. He was pacing just steps from his throne. His hands were in constant movement, scratching at his cheeks and neck. Every part of his body felt inflamed with irritation. His mind was infected with uncertainty and panic. He couldn't understand it. Even his throne was a source of severe agitation. It was as though the seat were lined with invisible, razor-thin shards. Every attempt to sit in his rightful place had him jumping up in pain.

And the floral scent leaking from the ornate structure left him baffled. For though it would be heavenly to some, it was toxic to Kingsley. It proclaimed the breach of his kingdom, the seepage from the outside world that in every imagining should have been impossible.

Just then, three faces peered in through his balcony.

"Mmm, it smells so good in here!" Mary exclaimed dreamily.

Kingsley stiffened. "How did you get in here!?" he snarled.

Christian held up his golden rope as he politely said, "Sorry for the intrusion. May we come in?"

Kingsley shook his head, confounded at their appearance.

Mary held up her hand in an effort to calm the wild, disoriented creature in front of them.

"There's a lot to explain," she admitted. "But the bottom line is that we've rescued most of your prisoners, and we won't be leaving here until everyone has been released."

Kingsley looked sickened by her words but managed to produce a menacing laugh. "They won't want to go. They have no one to go to. They were alone in the outside world." He looked down at his feet, before spitting out, "As was I, when I was just a child."

"You weren't alone," Joachim said softly. He pulled out a small, wooden item from his satchel. It was the toy car he had found in the cabin. He tentatively approached the old man, holding up the item as a tender offering.

Kingsley was shocked. He held the car, gently turning it over in his hands. "Where did you get this?" he whispered.

Joachim searched Kingsley's face. "It was from your mother, right?"

"It was destroyed."

"Maybe it was protected, so you could be reminded that someone really loved you," Joachim submitted. "A mother's love can be really powerful."

Just then, Kingsley's throne began to rattle. It seemed to be stretching, as though something was trying to burst out from within. Kingsley and his visitors stared in astonishment.

POOF! A rose popped into view. It had broken through the woven roots at the center of the throne. POOF! POOF! Another appeared, and another. The wooden seams were stretched apart as more flowers broke through, compromising the structure.

The strong aroma of roses saturated the space, as the beautiful flora continued to erupt through the knotted roots, until the throne looked as though it were covered by a rich, lush tapestry.

"I don't...I don't...I don't understand." Kingsley stammered.

St. John Henry seemed to appear out of nowhere. "My poor man, how ever did you come to believe that you should be able to build a kingdom devoid of the one true foundation?" He sighed. "This dominion of yours is perishing like a house built on sand. You sought to take ownership of that which was never yours to claim. At this very moment, the symbol of your alliance with demonic beings is being reordered to God. What you see here is the spiritual manifestation of the reality within the physical world."

Mary couldn't help interrupting. "I don't understand what you mean. What's happening in the physical world?"

"The demonstration of a maternal love is countering the deplorable hate that once claimed its stake in the forest outside the castle," the saint informed her. He clarified, "Your aunts have fulfilled their mission. They have brought your mother and grandmother and Father McCranager to the original location of Kingsley's treacherous allegiance. They are standing there as we speak. They have placed the image of Our Lady upon the throne and are consecrating the land to the Mystical Rose." He turned back to the defeated doctor. "Your kingdom is falling away."

Kingsley sneered in disgust, "I still have minds trapped here. Are you completely sure you are not putting them in danger?"

"I will ask you to join me on your balcony, if you would not mind terribly," the saint replied.

Kingsley's curiosity led him outside. The children joined them. In the distance, they could see a large cross upon a hill, surrounded by several figures. A small red light had been ignited.

. . .

Serena's head was lowered in prayer. Her stone was emitting a beautiful if rather subdued glow. She whispered the words St. John Henry Newman had composed:

"O my God, I confess that thou canst enlighten my darkness. I confess that thou alone canst. I wish my darkness to be enlightened...."

Liam was soon at her side.

"Allora, Serena, and I will need to get up higher," he determined after surveying the area.

Angelica pulled her stone from its chain. "I can help with that," she said excitedly.

Liam instructed his two sisters to join him just in front of the cross.

Angelica placed her stone on the ground and silently prayed. The rock seemed to flatten out, spreading and growing into a huge disk, large enough to accommodate the three siblings.

"Step on, guys!" Angelica called out. "I'm sending you on a ride." The three children complied, and Angelica then placed her hand just to the side of the platform. She lowered her head in earnest prayer as the rock began to vibrate and rumble. "Hold on!" she shouted. "To what?!" Allora shouted back.

"I don't know," she admitted. "I guess to each other?"

The rock continued to shake, then shot up into the air. The three siblings were knocked off their feet and clung to each other as they continued to rise. The towering boulder grew to such a height that it pierced through the low-lying clouds. Angelica took a step back, looking up and shaking her head as she flashed a proud, goofy smile.

Atop the great formation, Allora and the others were a little queasy from the surge. Liam quickly recovered and was soon all business. "Serena, find the prayers we need to free the lingering souls. Allora shine your light through the heart."

"I will," she said, "But we've done this before and I can tell you that my light can only expand so far. I don't think it will be able to reach everywhere."

"That's where I come in," he said with a smile. "I believe my glass can magnify the light."

"It's definitely worth a try," she said, hopeful that they were equipped to fulfill the task.

Serena bowed her head in prayer. The heart began to glow. Allora opened her locket, lifting it to shine through the heart. Liam raised his glass holding it just in front of the gem. Sure enough, the bright red beam shot through the night sky. Liam directed the flow of light, allowing it to shine to the very edge of the labyrinth. Slowly, the group rotated, like a lighthouse, sweeping the beam across the entire perimeter.

Serena's words poured out as a prayer to the Holy Spirit:

"O God, before whom every heart lies open, to whom every will speaks, and from whom no secret is hidden, purify, we beseech thee, our hearts by the inpouring of the Holy Spirit, that we may come to love thee perfectly and praise thee worthily. Through Christ Our Lord. Amen."

Will was below with Angelica, holding his crest. He could hear the hearts of many of the lingering children, aligning themselves to the prayer. They began to rise into the air, like dew absorbed by the morning light.

Serena broke into a psalm:

"Now that I am old and gray, do not forsake me, God, that I may proclaim your might to all generations yet to come... once more revive me. From the watery depths of the earth once more raise me up. Restore my honor; turn and comfort me."

Angelica looked at Will, whose smile was alive with joy and highly infectious. "Wow," he whispered. "Those words are clearing out every last one of Kingsley's prisoners." Angelica looked out, taking in the full scope of the area. Will was right: everywhere she looked there were shafts of light rising to great heights before disappearing altogether.

Serena wasn't finished. She broke into one final prayer, it was a consecration prayer to the Mystical Rose, and as it swept over the land, the very walls became as fragrant petals, fluttering and softly floating up into the air, red and ripe with graces.

Angelica and Will raised their hands as the rush of delicate blessings flickered over their arms and faces. They began to slowly sink down. The mountain beneath their feet began releasing a flurry of lush flora. The red petals swirled around the cross, lifting to the sky. Angelica couldn't help thinking that it was the perfect image: red droplets ascending from the cross, as prayers to the heavens.

Back in Kingsley's wooden cave, the fallen king stared out in horror. "This cannot be," he muttered, his features displaying his utter, dismal shock. The pale-green fog filling his kingdom swirled into a fragrant, pinkish mist and lifted into the sky.

St. John Henry released a glorious sigh. "The cloud is lifted forever."

Kingsley's shoulders sank as he lowered his head in

defeat. Suddenly he gasped, lifting his trembling hands in bewilderment. There was a noticeable transparency; they seemed to be fading. "What is happening to me?" he cried.

"Your world has been reclaimed. You no longer have a place here," the saint replied. "We will soon see you back in the physical world, but mark my words well: never again will you be permitted to prey on souls."

"Will we be evaporating too?" Christian asked with wide eyes.

"No," the saint replied. "This world is passing away, but we will exit as we entered: with our bodies intact."

Kingsley began to dissipate, floating up into the atmosphere. St. John Henry smiled and bid him adieu. "Away with you, Kingsley. It seems your time to fly into space has arrived."

CHAPTER 33

Kingsley's groggy eyes opened to the glossy faces towering over him. He pressed his hand to the very top of his head and let out a weary moan. He looked at his hand and scrunched up his face in disgust at the glittery residue.

"Good morning," Pam said, bending over and staring him square in the eyes.

Kingsley sat up, surprised to find himself on the sofa in the Great Room. Pam straightened up. At her side were Sophia, Roger Keble, and two police officers. One of the officers dangled a set of handcuffs before Kingsley, who was striving to compose himself.

"What is the meaning of this?" he demanded to know.

Keble held up several folders. "We found these in your office. They are copies of your patient's trust account statements. It is clear that you were withdrawing funds without their consent. There are also lists of prescription drugs that you had been administering to your patients—again, without their consent. Every patient in the east wing has been violated in some manner."

"Sophia, and many, many others have regained their ability to communicate," Pam informed him, "and with clear minds, they have been able to share about the mental abuse they endured through your attempts to belittle and manipulate them. Some patients' family members were not permitted to visit them: a violation of their rights. There are even stolen articles from the patients that were found in your office."

"It's over, Dr. Kingsley," Keble assured him. "You will be facing justice."

Just then, the children entered the room, dressed in their regular attire, accompanied by the saint, the aunts, and several of the children's family members.

The doctor wrinkled his nose and stared at the saint with a look of repugnance.

Mary couldn't help getting a little emotional thinking of all the people who had been hurt by Kingsley's actions.

With tears in her eyes, she admonished the old man, "My heart aches for your victims."

Kingsley rolled his eyes and huffed in frustration. "Don't you see? I am a victim. No one has suffered as I have. Robbed of the land and wealth to which I was entitled. A child subjected to horrendous poverty. All of my actions were justified in attempting to restore what was owed to me."

The saint sighed. "Claiming to be a victim is never a justification for evil acts or harming others. You have destroyed lives, and the fact that you believe your actions to be justified only exposes your selfishness and total disregard for the dignity and humanity of those around you. A mindset such as yours infects the land; it spreads its lies until it siphons the life and goodness out of everything it touches." The saint's frown softened, as he looked deeply into the old man's eyes. "But hope remains, Kingsley. In spite of everything, you are not a lost cause. I pray you will change...and change often."

The officers read the doctor his rights and cuffed him. As they began to lead him away, Aunt Dolly, who was near the back of the group, cried out, "Oh Georgie, how could you have been so cruel?" She sniffed. "And to think I already ordered my wedding gown."

She lowered her head, but not before sweeping her eyes over Roger Keble's hands, in search of a wedding ring.

. . .

The sun was infusing the falls with intense light, sending a rainbow up through the mist.

Allora held her little sister Kiara's hand, as they counted to three and jumped from the very top, plummeting into the pool beneath and splashing their four brothers. As Allora broke through the surface, she found herself searching for Will. She soon caught his eye. He was seated on a boulder with an older woman with large brown eyes at his side. He mouthed the words, "It's Rachel," pointing to the woman with a huge smile on his face.

There were many seniors enjoying the property. Aunt Dot stood behind a picnic table garnished with a rich spread of fruit and fresh baked pastries. She added a large bowl of leafy salad to the mix, before giving Aunt Frankie an imperious look. Aunt Frankie lifted an eyebrow in response as she approached her sister, still clenching her wooden spoon. Aunt Dot looked a little nervous, but soon breathed a sigh of relief as Frankie revealed the large wooden fork she'd been hiding behind her back. She placed the two utensils in the salad bowl and the two sisters laughed. "Oh, YOU!" Aunt Dot said, giving her sister a playful swat.

Aunt Dolly was gracefully frolicking along a pathway with Roger Keble. It seemed her broken heart was quickly on the mend. Mary and Serena ran past them, followed by a slew of their giggling younger siblings. Angelica sat in the shade of a tree with her friends Edward and Violet—but not the tree with poison ivy at its base. No one wanted a rash on their woddler.

The children's grandmother, mother, and father stood on the bridge. The proud parents were holding baby Avila and little Lucy, gazing at the spread of blessings before them.

"It is such a gift to be back here again with my sisters," the silvery-blonde-haired woman exclaimed, with smiling eyes. "And the atmosphere here has never been more heavenly." Unbeknownst to them, they were joined by a saintly guest, who was hidden from their sight but readily extending them his blessing.

The children and Will all sensed the presence on the bridge, and looked in his direction. He raised his hand and blessed them. He looked deeply pleased, but also a little sad. Serena and Mary couldn't keep the tears from flowing down their cheeks, as they realized that it was their humble friend's way of saying goodbye. They hoped he could sense their deep gratitude. They watched as he faded out of sight. "I can't wait till our next mission," Serena said to her sister.

"I can wait maybe a little bit," Mary admitted. "I think I need a few sessions of hot tea and cucumber sandwiches to help heal my heart."

Aunt Frankie approached Mary and placed her hand gently on her shoulder. "Are you okay?" she asked, noticing Mary's red eyes. Mary sighed as she whispered, "Goodbyes are just really, really hard sometimes."

Aunt Frankie's eyes became misty. She seemed a little embarrassed, but quickly pulled her niece into a hug. "I know," she admitted, amidst uncharacteristically tearful sniffles. Mary waited for the series of five quick pats to end the hug.

But they never came.

THE END

ST. JOHN HENRY NEWMAN WAS BORN ON February 21, 1801 in London, England. He was the eldest of six children, and his father was a banker, but when the bank failed, he managed a brewery. Newman was an Anglican, who converted to Evangelical Calvinism in his teenage years. In 1825, he became an Anglican priest, and in 1845, after many years of seeking the truth, he converted to Catholicism. In 1879, he was made a Cardinal. St. John Henry Newman died on August 11, 1890, at the age of 89.

Here are 10 facts about St. Cardinal John Henry Newman:

1. In 1808, seven-year-old John Henry was sent to a boarding school in London. During the summer, he felt very lonely and became ill. While reading religious books, he had a strong spiritual encounter where he knew, without a doubt, that God was absolutely real and very close to him.

2. St. John Henry was a great writer who produced over 30 published works in his lifetime.
3. His motto (used on his coat of arms as Cardinal) was Cor ad cor loquitor, which means "heart speaks to heart". This saying was inspired by a letter written by St. Francis de Sales, and perfectly captured his genuine love for those he encountered.
4. St. John Henry was known for his keen intellect and also for his warmth and kindness. He had a great love for souls and a special devotion to the poor and the elderly.
5. St. John Henry wrote the hymn "Lead Kindly Light," as well as two other hymns called "Firmly I Believe, and Truly," and "Praise to the Holiest in the Height." The last two hymns were originally written into a poem he wrote called "The Dream of Gerontius."
6. Some priests did not like St. John Henry Newman. Some tried to ruin his reputation, which became a great sadness for him. However, most of this ended once he became a cardinal, at which point, through tears of joy, he exclaimed, "The cloud is lifted forever."
7. St. John Henry Newman died on August 11, 1890 at the age of 89. However, since that day was already the feast day of St. Clare of Assisi, the Catholic Church decided that his feast day should be on October 9 instead. This date is around the start of the university year which is fitting because St. John Henry had a special love for

universities and the formation of students. He even helped to found the first Catholic University in Ireland.

8. St. John Henry chose to put the Latin words *Ex Umbris et Imaginibus in Veritatem*, which means "Out of Shadows and Images and Into the Truth," on his tombstone.
9. The two miracles that led to St. John Henry Newman's canonization were the healing of a deacon from a spinal injury in 2001 and the healing of a pregnant woman in 2018. Both of these miracles were attributed to his intercession.
10. There was a man named Dr. Charles Kingsley, an Anglican preacher, who began a debate with Fr. John Henry when he wrongly attributed a quote as being the words of the holy priest. The debate went on for a long time, until Fr. John Henry wrote, "Away with you, Mr. Kingsley, and fly into space." Then Fr. John Henry wrote Apologia Pro Vita Sua, which in English means "A Defense of One's Own Life," defending his opinions and beliefs.